First published in 1984
Usborne Publishing Ltd
Usborne House, 83-85 Saffron Hill
London EC1N 8RT

© Usborne Publishing Ltd
1984

American edition 1984.

The name of Usborne and the device 😊 are Trade Marks of Usborne Publishing Ltd.

Printed in Scotland

About this book

This is a most unusual and exciting dictionary of pictures for the whole family. It contains over 2,700 words grouped into interesting thematic topics.

Younger children will use Wordfinder as a picture book. If shared with an enthusiastic adult it will help to extend their vocabulary and encourage careful observation. In time these children will also be able to match pictures to the printed word.

For older children this delightful book presents many opportunities for enjoyment and learning. They will use it to gain information and to help them with their writing and spelling.

Because there is so much detail in all the beautifully drawn pictures, children will wish to return to this book again and again, learning something new each time.

The alphabetical index at the back of this book will encourage children to look up words and then find the right page and picture.

Finding words in Wordfinder will give endless pleasure to children of all ages.

Betty Root
Centre for the Teaching of Reading
University of Reading, England

In this book, you will sometimes see a word in **heavy type**, such as **103**, **living room** , on page 7. This word refers to part of the picture on that page. The words that follow it are all things you might find in a **living room** , such as bookcase, stereo, sofa or television. On the picture the numbers inside two circles, like this ⑩③, refer to the words in **heavy type**.

THE USBORNE
CHILDREN'S
WORDFINDER

Anne Civardi
Illustrated by Colin King

Consultant: Betty Root
Series Editor: Heather Amery

With thanks to Lynn Bresler

The building site

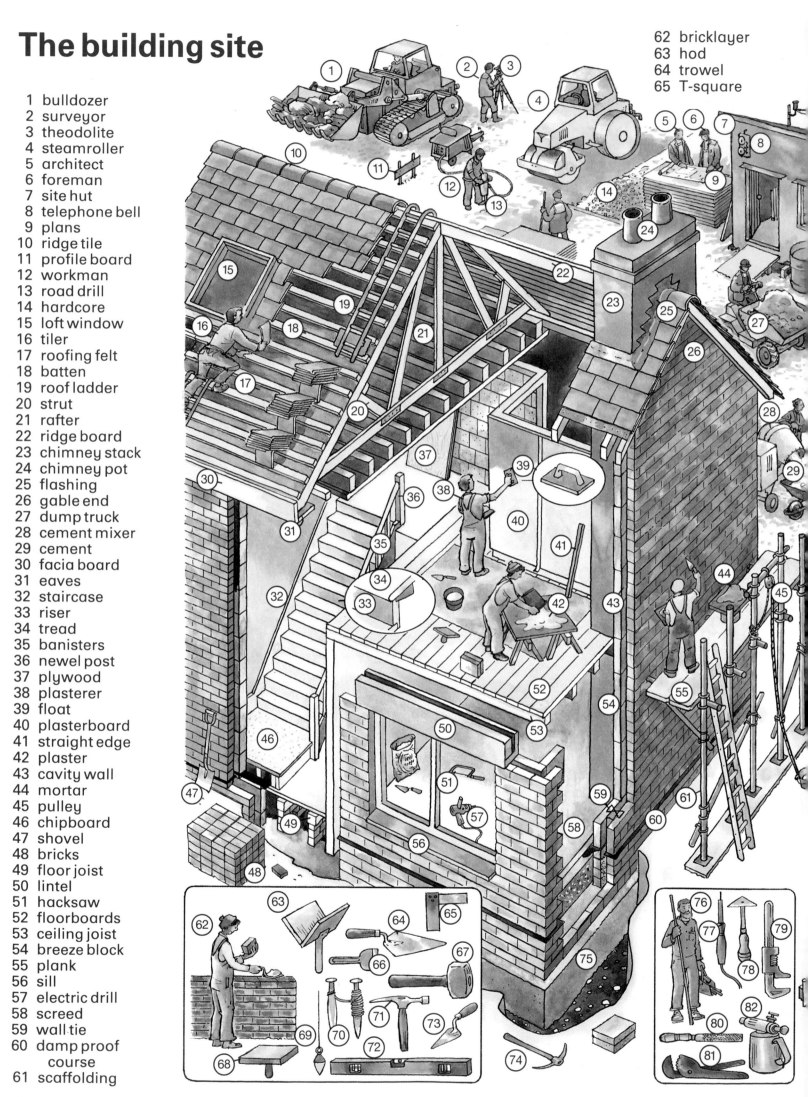

1 bulldozer
2 surveyor
3 theodolite
4 steamroller
5 architect
6 foreman
7 site hut
8 telephone bell
9 plans
10 ridge tile
11 profile board
12 workman
13 road drill
14 hardcore
15 loft window
16 tiler
17 roofing felt
18 batten
19 roof ladder
20 strut
21 rafter
22 ridge board
23 chimney stack
24 chimney pot
25 flashing
26 gable end
27 dump truck
28 cement mixer
29 cement
30 facia board
31 eaves
32 staircase
33 riser
34 tread
35 banisters
36 newel post
37 plywood
38 plasterer
39 float
40 plasterboard
41 straight edge
42 plaster
43 cavity wall
44 mortar
45 pulley
46 chipboard
47 shovel
48 bricks
49 floor joist
50 lintel
51 hacksaw
52 floorboards
53 ceiling joist
54 breeze block
55 plank
56 sill
57 electric drill
58 screed
59 wall tie
60 damp proof course
61 scaffolding

62 bricklayer
63 hod
64 trowel
65 T-square

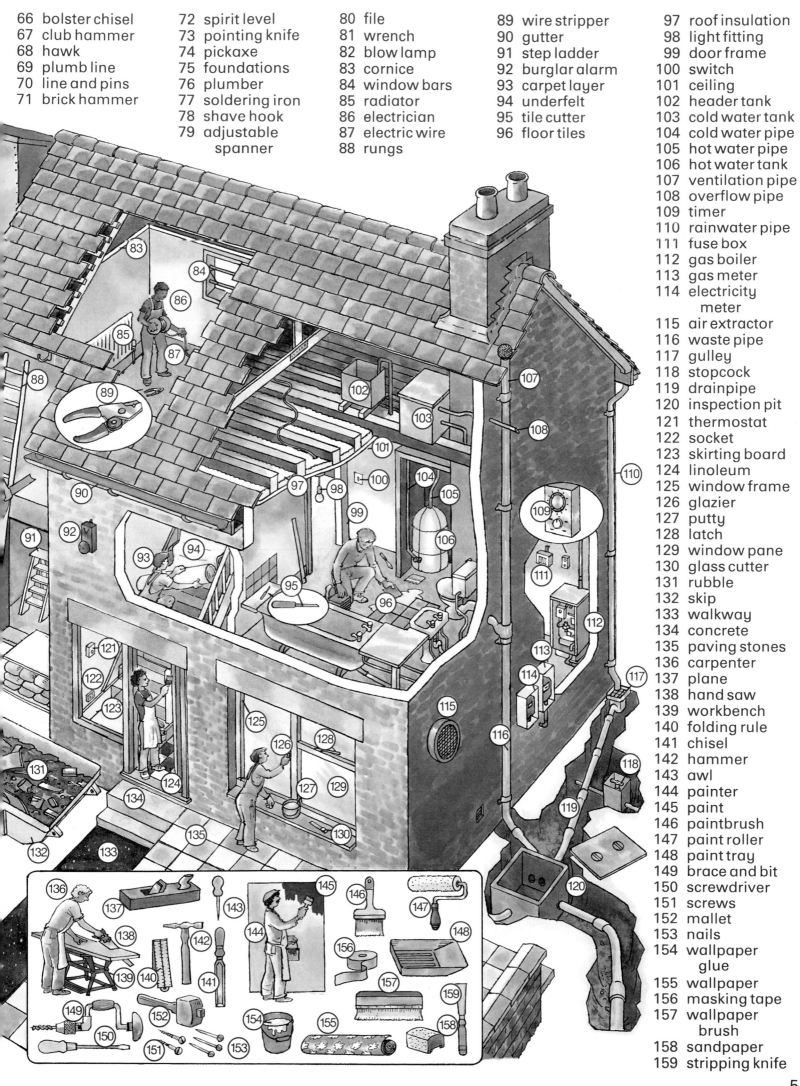

66 bolster chisel
67 club hammer
68 hawk
69 plumb line
70 line and pins
71 brick hammer

72 spirit level
73 pointing knife
74 pickaxe
75 foundations
76 plumber
77 soldering iron
78 shave hook
79 adjustable spanner

80 file
81 wrench
82 blow lamp
83 cornice
84 window bars
85 radiator
86 electrician
87 electric wire
88 rungs

89 wire stripper
90 gutter
91 step ladder
92 burglar alarm
93 carpet layer
94 underfelt
95 tile cutter
96 floor tiles

97 roof insulation
98 light fitting
99 door frame
100 switch
101 ceiling
102 header tank
103 cold water tank
104 cold water pipe
105 hot water pipe
106 hot water tank
107 ventilation pipe
108 overflow pipe
109 timer
110 rainwater pipe
111 fuse box
112 gas boiler
113 gas meter
114 electricity meter
115 air extractor
116 waste pipe
117 gulley
118 stopcock
119 drainpipe
120 inspection pit
121 thermostat
122 socket
123 skirting board
124 linoleum
125 window frame
126 glazier
127 putty
128 latch
129 window pane
130 glass cutter
131 rubble
132 skip
133 walkway
134 concrete
135 paving stones
136 carpenter
137 plane
138 hand saw
139 workbench
140 folding rule
141 chisel
142 hammer
143 awl
144 painter
145 paint
146 paintbrush
147 paint roller
148 paint tray
149 brace and bit
150 screwdriver
151 screws
152 mallet
153 nails
154 wallpaper glue
155 wallpaper
156 masking tape
157 wallpaper brush
158 sandpaper
159 stripping knife

5

The house

1 television aerial
2 roof
3 **attic**
4 boxes
5 cot
6 trunk

7 lampshade
8 lampstand
9 playpen
10 bulb
11 high chair
12 **bedroom**

13 curtain rail
14 striplight
15 mirror
16 father
17 wardrobe
18 curtain

6

19 headboard	25 shirt	31 cushion	36 towel ring
20 sheet	26 comforter	32 chest of drawers	37 medicine cabinet
21 alarm clock	27 bedside table	**33 bathroom**	38 toilet paper
22 dressing table	28 blanket	34 linen closet	39 towel
23 lamp	29 slippers	35 shower	40 taps
24 pillow	30 bed		41 son

41 son
42 washbasin
43 bath
44 bathroom scales
45 bathmat
46 toilet
47 laundry basket
48 vase
49 door
50 grandfather clock
51 hamster
52 mother
53 patchwork quilt
54 vacuum cleaner
55 daughter
56 rocking chair
57 bunkbeds
58 fish tank
59 window box
60 porch
61 kitchen
62 chimes
63 door bell
64 cat flap
65 bone
66 dog bowl
67 tumble dryer
68 bird cage
69 kitchen cabinet
70 worktop
71 sink
72 blind
73 draining board
74 grandmother
75 oven
76 dishwasher
77 tray
78 washing machine
79 refrigerator
80 freezer
81 dresser
82 fruit bowl
83 iron
84 ironing board
85 tablecloth
86 table
87 stool
88 garbage can
89 bread board
90 place mat
91 glass
92 napkin
93 milk jug
94 chair
95 dog basket
96 umbrella stand

97 portrait
98 hall
99 coat rack
100 telephone
101 telephone directories
102 doormat
103 living room
104 bookcase
105 photograph frame
106 record deck
107 stereo
108 sofa
109 grandfather
110 shelf
111 magazine rack
112 window
113 television
114 armchair
115 coffee table
116 ashtray
117 rug
118 wastepaper basket
119 toothbrush
120 soap
121 toothpaste
122 bath salts
123 cup
124 saucer
125 comb
126 hair brush
127 shampoo
128 plate
129 soup bowl
130 dust rag
131 polish
132 dustpan
133 scrubbing brush
134 teapot
135 coffee pot
136 detergent
137 sugar bowl
138 butter dish
139 toaster
140 can opener
141 blender
142 knife
143 fork
144 spoon
145 toast rack
146 carving knife
147 carving fork
148 corkscrew
149 egg timer
150 saucepan
151 frying pan
152 casserole dish
153 ladle
154 salt-cellar
155 peppermill
156 candlestick
157 colander
158 kettle

7

Sports I

1 starting block
2 sprinter
3 track shoe
4 athlete
5 stadium
6 running track
7 arena
8 spectators
9 coach
10 marathon runner
11 starting gun
12 competitors
13 winner
14 finishing line
15 water jump
16 steeplechaser
17 hurdler
18 hurdle
19 long jump
20 high jump
21 crossbar
22 take-off board
23 triple jump
24 pole vault
25 race walker
26 javelin
27 discus thrower
28 shot put
29 safety cage
30 hammer thrower
31 relay race
32 baton
33 discs
34 barbell
35 weightlifter
36 wrestling boots
37 wrestler
38 contestant
39 flight
40 dart
41 darts player
42 scorer
43 scoreboard
44 dartboard
45 karate
46 high kick
47 karate suit
48 judo
49 black belt
50 judoka
51 boxing
52 headguard
53 boxer
54 referee
55 boxing ring
56 corner cushion
57 judge
58 time keeper
59 gong
60 manager
61 second
62 speedball

63 punchbag
64 punchball
65 dumb bell

66 fencing
67 fencing mask
68 fencing master

69 swordsman
70 half-jacket
71 breeches

72 foil
73 fencing glove
74 cuff

86 trampoline
87 rings
88 parallel bars
89 horizontal bar
90 pommel horse
91 instructor
92 wall bars
93 headstand
94 bench
95 landing mat
96 somersault
97 mattress
98 handstand
99 rope
100 golf
101 golf clubs
102 golf bag
103 teeing ground
104 golfer
105 golf trolley
106 caddie
107 tee
108 fairway
109 golf ball
110 putting green
111 flagstick
112 bunker
113 rough
114 club house
115 waterskier
116 waterskis
117 jumping ramp
118 tow rope
119 motor boat
120 tennis
121 umpire
122 linesman
123 tennis court
124 baseline
125 tramlines
126 doubles
    sideline
127 singles sideline
128 service line
129 tennis net
130 ballboy
131 server
132 tennis racket
133 grip
134 tennis ball
135 rollerskater
136 rollerskate
137 toe binding
138 toe stop
139 elbow pad
140 kick tail
141 knee pad
142 skateboard
143 high board
144 diver
145 swimming pool
146 diving board
147 lanes
148 backstroke
149 starter
150 bathing cap

75 épée
76 sabre
77 gymnast
78 vaulting horse
79 gymnasium
80 leotard
81 beam
82 asymmetric
   bars
83 vaulting box
84 springboard
85 buck

9

Sports II

1 **skiing**
2 ski jump
3 mountain
4 cable car
5 chair lift
6 skier
7 piste
8 ski class
9 ski instructor
10 toboggan
11 slalom course
12 ski

13 ski boot
14 ski pole
15 **American football**
16 shoulder pad
17 thigh pad
18 goal post
19 **soccer**
20 corner flag
21 striker
22 soccer ball
23 whistle

24 **cricket**
25 fielder
26 batsman
27 cricket bat
28 wicket keeper
29 cricket pad
30 bowler
31 cricket ball
32 stumps
33 bowling crease
34 batting glove
35 **rugby**

93 bowling mat
94 bowling green
95 bowl
96 jack
97 **table tennis**
98 table tennis bat

99 center line
100 **rifle shooting**
101 optical sight
102 rifle
103 marksman
104 cartridges

105 rifle range
106 **boules**
107 boule
108 baguette
109 pitch
110 **squash**

111 squash court
112 squash ball
113 squash racket
114 service box
115 **archery**
116 bowstring

117 bow
118 shaft
119 arm bracer
120 target
121 bull's eye
122 **croquet**

36 scrum	48 base	59 racing colors	71 triple bar	82 brakeman
37 scrum half	49 pitcher's	60 racehorse	72 horse jump	83 captain
38 rugby ball	mound	61 whip	73 riding boot	84 two-man
39 lacrosse	50 pitcher	62 jockey	74 jodhpurs	bobsleigh
40 crosse	**51 ice hockey**	63 blinkers	75 riding hat	85 front runner
41 baseball	52 ice skate	64 winning post	**76 surfing**	**86 curling**
42 catcher	53 stick glove	**65 canoeing**	77 skeg	87 curling broom
43 baseball bat	54 goal pad	66 kayak	78 surfboard	88 skip (captain)
44 batter	55 goal line	67 bowman	79 surf leash	89 target circle
45 mitt	56 goal crease	68 deck	**80 bobsleigh**	90 rink
46 home plate	57 puck	**69 show jumping**	racing	91 curling stone
47 outfielder	**58 horse racing**	70 post-and-rails	81 rear runner	**92 bowls**

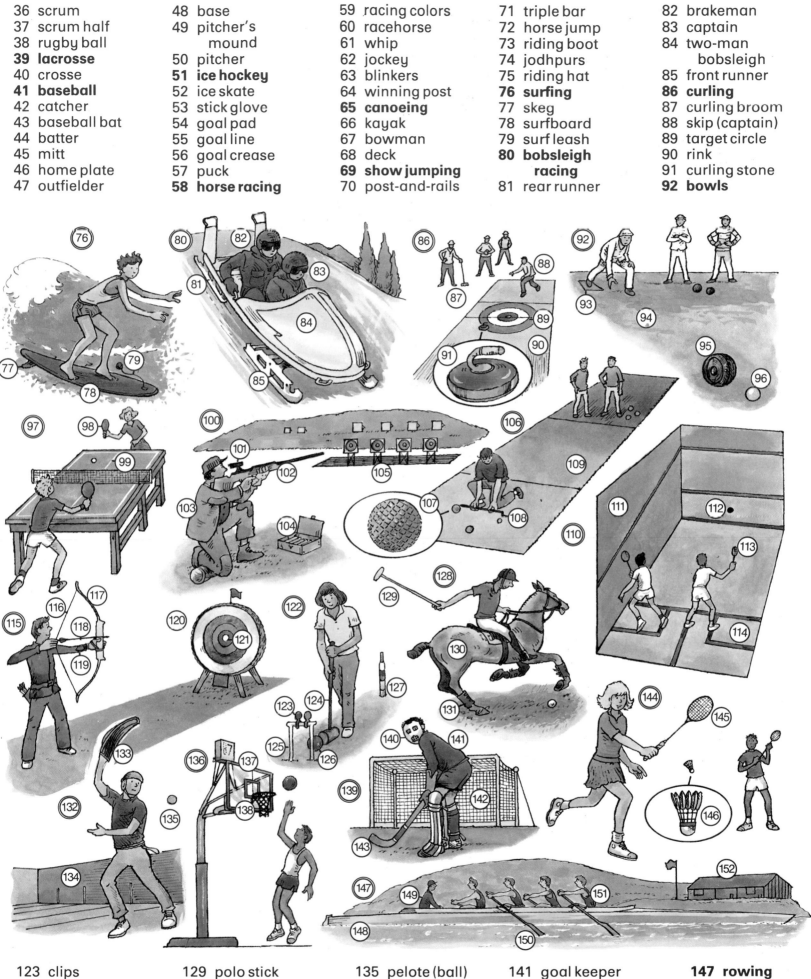

123 clips	129 polo stick	135 pelote (ball)	141 goal keeper	**147 rowing**
124 croquet mallet	130 polo pony	**136 basketball**	142 goal	148 skiff
125 hoop	131 ankle bandage	137 backboard	143 hockey stick	149 cox
126 croquet ball	**132 jai-alai**	138 basket rim	**144 badminton**	150 oar
127 winning peg	133 cesta (basket)	**139 hockey**	145 badminton racket	151 oarsman
128 polo	134 jai-alai court	140 faceguard	146 shuttlecock	152 boat house

On the farm

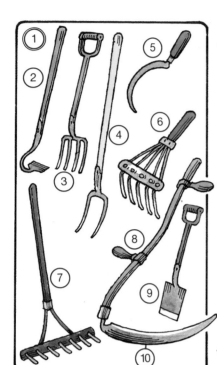

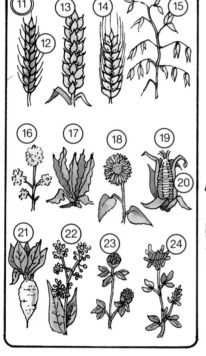

1 tools	16 mustard	31 lamb	46 mowing machine	61 rain barrel
2 hoe	17 kale	32 ewe	47 hen house	62 bird table
3 digging fork	18 sunflower	33 ram	48 feeder	63 wall
4 pitchfork	19 maize	34 boar	49 hare	64 hose
5 sickle	20 cob	35 snout	50 shed	65 kennel
6 potato rake	21 sugar beet	36 sow	51 hay net	66 puppies
7 hay rake	22 rape	37 piglet	52 stable	67 mud
8 scythe	23 clover	38 field	53 farmhouse	68 rabbit
9 spade	24 alfalfa	39 shelter	54 shutter	69 rabbit hutch
10 blade	25 cow	40 paddock	55 kitten	70 farmer's wife
11 crops	26 udder	41 gate	56 cat	71 eggs
12 rye	27 calf	42 bees	57 pigsty	72 fence
13 wheat	28 tail	43 beehive	58 trough	73 reeds
14 barley	29 bull	44 tractor	59 broom	74 pond
15 oats	30 nose ring	45 hedge	60 boots	75 peacock

76 nanny goat	91 beak	106 sacks	121 milk tanker	136 roller
77 kid	92 hen	107 hedge cutter	122 milk	**137 farm machinery**
78 horn	93 scarecrow	108 farmer	123 dairy	138 forage
79 billy goat	94 furrows	109 corn	124 horse	harvester
80 mare	95 haystack	110 workshop	125 mane	139 combine
81 foal	96 silo	111 cowshed	126 saddle	harvester
82 donkey	97 shepherd	112 stall	127 horse rider	140 hay baler
83 duck	98 sheep dog	113 straw	128 reins	141 seed drill
84 duckling	99 sheep	114 hayloft	129 stirrup	142 cultivator
85 carthorse	100 weathervane	115 rat	130 hoof	143 harrow
86 turkey	101 sheep dip	116 ladder	131 fertilizer	144 plough
87 goose	102 fruit picker	117 barn owl	132 overall	145 manure
88 gosling	103 orchard	118 farm worker	133 dairyman	146 manure spreader
89 cockerel	104 cattle grid	119 farm manager	134 milking machine	147 hay elevator
90 feathers	105 barn	120 hay bale	135 trailer	148 potato harvester

13

At the airport

1 **instrument panel**
2 artificial horizon
3 airspeed indicator
4 altimeter
5 radio compass
6 boost gauge
7 tachometer
8 temperature gauge
9 turn indicator
10 control stick
11 throttle lever
12 rudder pedal
13 **light aircraft**
14 propeller blade
15 spinner
16 cockpit cover
17 aileron
18 landing flap
19 **helicopter**
20 tail skid
21 stabilizer
22 tail rotor
23 exhaust outlet
24 rotor hub
25 rotor blade
26 skid landing gear
27 **jump jet**
28 outrigger wheel
29 tail puffer
30 airbrake
31 fan air nozzle
32 pitot head
33 wheel well
34 **airship**
35 nose cone
36 gas bags
37 skycrane
38 **supersonic airliner**
39 droop nose
40 turbo-prop
41 executive jet
42 glider
43 **seaplane**
44 seawing
45 float
46 **freight plane**
47 hinged nose
48 **airport**
49 car park
50 radio aerial
51 floodlights
52 radar
53 control tower
54 ground control officer

55 flight plan
56 observation terrace
57 passenger bridge
58 cargo container
59 **jet plane**
60 elevator
61 tailcone
62 rudder
63 tail fin
64 national flag
65 tailplane
66 registration number
67 cargo hold
68 washroom
69 food trolley
70 bulkhead
71 emergency exit

72 reclining seats
73 cinema screen
74 antenna
75 supervisor's van
76 spoiler
77 wing tip
78 windsock
79 runway lights
80 runway
81 anti-collision light
82 passenger cabin
83 engine intake
84 flight engineer
85 co-pilot
86 pilot
87 flight deck
88 airport police car
89 marshaller
90 earmuffs
91 radome
92 nose wheels
93 landing light
94 stewardess
95 fuselage
96 undercarriage
97 jet engine
98 engine cowling
99 maintenance engineer
100 passenger terminal
101 duty free shop
102 departure gate
103 security check
104 departure lounge
105 passport
106 airline ticket
107 boarding pass
108 hand luggage
109 flight indicator board
110 conveyor belt
111 check-in desk
112 departure hall
113 flight information
114 airport official
115 hotel reservations
116 car rental
117 arrivals hall
118 customs control
119 luggage carousel
120 luggage reclaim hall
121 immigration officer
122 passport control
123 moving walkway
124 airport vehicles
125 refueller
126 freshwater tanker
127 air conditioning vehicle
128 mobile generator
129 baggage train
130 snow blower
131 cherry picker
132 scissor-lift transporter
133 lavatory cleaning vehicle
134 crew bus
135 ice removal vehicle
136 passenger bus
137 tow truck
138 fire tender

15

The beach and the sea

1 cave
2 beach café
3 megaphone
4 telescope
5 lifeguard
6 changing room
7 ice cream stall
8 pedal boat
9 shrimper
10 bollard
11 lifebelt
12 promenade
13 windbreak
14 sun hat
15 umbrella
16 shrimping net
17 seal
18 seal pup
19 tideline
20 cormorant
21 swimming
   trunks
22 wing
23 beach bag
24 picnic hamper
25 beach towel
26 deckchair
27 sand
28 beachball
29 armband
30 cuttlefish
31 rock
32 bucket
33 sandcastle
34 spade
35 **rock pool**
36 razor shells
37 sea squirts
38 tower shell
39 oysters
40 claw
41 crab
42 sea anemone
43 Portuguese-
   man-of-war
44 sea lettuce
45 barnacle
46 mussels
47 whelk
48 cockles
49 limpets
50 goose barnacle
51 spider crab
52 shrimp
53 sea slug
54 periwinkle
55 egg case
56 sea urchin
57 hermit crab
58 starfish
59 scallop
60 lobster

61 pincer
62 jellyfish
63 dolphin

64 fin
65 seaweed
66 ray

67 eel
68 sailfish
69 spines

70 swordfish
71 octopus
72 siphon

16

85 lifeboat station
86 slipway
87 lighthouse
88 bay
89 island
90 raft
91 snorkel
92 fish boxes
93 net
94 frisbee
95 breakwater
96 windsurfer
97 swimmer
98 buoy
99 sea
100 flipper
101 goggles
102 seagull
103 surf
104 lugworm
105 anchor
106 crab pot
107 post
108 lobster pot
109 jetty
110 driftwood
111 wave
112 fisherman
113 fishing boat
114 pipefish
115 seahorse
116 turtle
117 sawfish
118 giant clam
119 porpoise
120 sea serpent
121 shark
122 whale
123 frogman
124 underwater
    camera
125 coral
126 mini submarine
127 conning tower
128 navigator
129 ballast tank
130 cage
131 cable
132 shipwreck
133 speargun
134 weight belt
135 aqualung
136 sea scooter
137 wetsuit
138 depth gauge
139 waterproof
    watch
140 oxygen tube
141 deep sea diver
142 diving helmet
143 trench
144 bathyscaphe
145 pressure hull
146 acoustic probe
147 sea bed

73 suckers
74 tentacle
75 cuttlefish
76 diving saucer
77 water jet
78 searchlight
79 mechanical arm
80 squid
81 sponge
82 coast guard
83 sand dunes
84 fog signal

Food

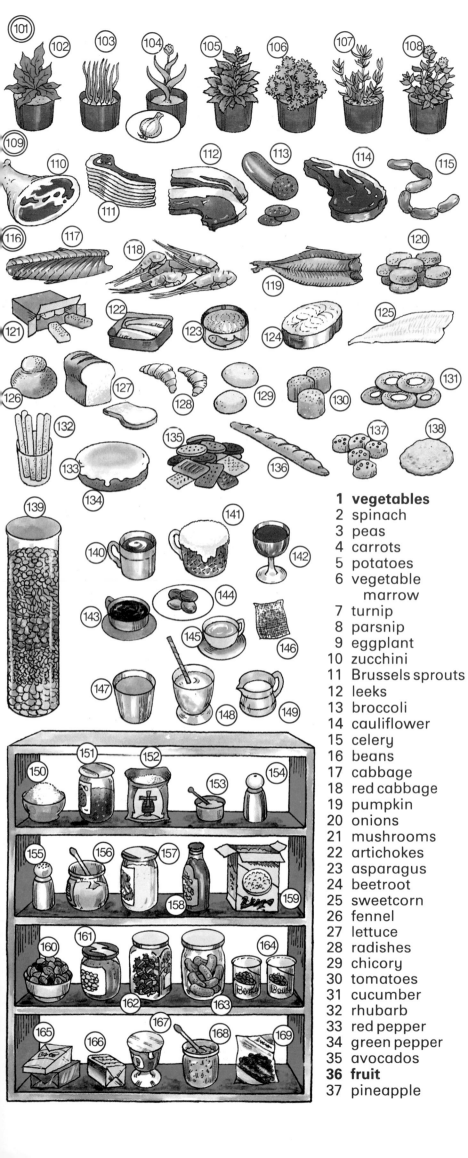

38 coconuts
39 bananas
40 grapes
41 limes
42 lemons
43 oranges
44 grapefruit
45 mangoes
46 paw paws
47 figs
48 pears
49 apples
50 tangerines
51 lychees
52 melons
53 water melons
54 peaches
55 plums
56 dates
57 apricots
58 greengages
59 redcurrants
60 blueberries
61 strawberries
62 raspberries
63 gooseberries
64 cranberries
65 blackberries
66 salad
67 stew
68 spaghetti
69 syrup
70 meat pie
71 rice
72 dumplings
73 soup
74 omelette
75 fried eggs
76 hamburger
77 pancakes
78 potato chips
79 hot dogs
80 roast turkey
81 stuffing
82 sandwiches
83 pizza
84 quiche
85 caviar
86 ice cream
87 pâté
88 chocolate sauce
89 soufflé
90 jelly
91 mousse
92 shish kebabs
93 éclairs
94 fruit salad
95 cheesecake
96 custard
97 pastry
98 meringues
99 fruit tart
100 trifle
101 herbs
102 basil
103 chives

104 garlic
105 mint
106 parsley
107 rosemary
108 thyme
109 meat
110 ham
111 bacon
112 chops
113 salami
114 steak
115 sausages
116 fish
117 smoked salmon
118 prawns
119 kippers
120 fish cakes
121 fish fingers
122 sardines
123 tuna fish
124 fish steak
125 fish filet
126 brown bread
127 white bread
128 croissants
129 bread rolls
130 muffins
131 doughnuts
132 breadsticks
133 icing
134 cake
135 cookies
136 French loaf
137 scones
138 pita bread
139 dried beans
140 hot chocolate
141 beer
142 wine
143 coffee
144 coffee beans
145 tea
146 teabag
147 fruit juice
148 milkshake
149 cream
150 sugar
151 jam
152 flour
153 mustard
154 salt
155 pepper
156 honey
157 mayonnaise
158 tomato ketchup
159 cereal
160 nuts
161 peanut butter
162 candies
163 gherkins
164 baked beans
165 cheese
166 butter
167 yoghurt
168 marmalade
169 raisins

1 vegetables
2 spinach
3 peas
4 carrots
5 potatoes
6 vegetable marrow
7 turnip
8 parsnip
9 eggplant
10 zucchini
11 Brussels sprouts
12 leeks
13 broccoli
14 cauliflower
15 celery
16 beans
17 cabbage
18 red cabbage
19 pumpkin
20 onions
21 mushrooms
22 artichokes
23 asparagus
24 beetroot
25 sweetcorn
26 fennel
27 lettuce
28 radishes
29 chicory
30 tomatoes
31 cucumber
32 rhubarb
33 red pepper
34 green pepper
35 avocados
36 fruit
37 pineapple

The castle

1 foot soldier
2 bill
3 kettle hat
4 pike
5 crossbow
6 stirrup
7 quarrel
8 trigger
9 quiver
10 arrows
11 longbow
12 axe
13 flail
14 mace
15 dagger
16 siege tower
17 battering ram
18 ballista
19 sling
20 trebuchet
21 mantlet
22 archer
23 mangonel
24 firepot
25 boiling oil
26 cannon
27 breech
28 touch hole
29 rope wad
30 cannon balls
31 gunpowder
    cartridge
32 muzzle
33 gun carriage
34 taper
35 rammer
36 knight
37 quilted vest
38 squire
39 leggings
40 hood
41 chain mail
42 scale armor
43 plate armor
44 basinet
45 breast plate
46 sabaton
47 roundel
48 tunic
49 great helm
50 coat-of-arms
51 sheath
52 broadsword
53 shin guard
54 lance
55 shield
56 jousting
    tournament
57 quintain
58 plume
59 pavilion
60 nobles

61 coronel
62 horse armor
63 tilt
64 pommel
    saddle
65 crest
66 trumpeters
67 herald
68 castle
69 turret
70 battlements
71 solar
72 keep
73 lancet window
74 baron
75 tailor
76 baroness
77 maid
78 tapestry
79 chaplain
80 cross
81 chapel
82 troubadour
83 pallet
84 gallery
85 minstrel
86 tub
87 candle
88 great hall
89 fireplace
90 spiral staircase
91 barrel
92 dungeon
93 prisoner
94 ball and chain
95 jailer
96 garderobe
97 bench
98 trestle table
99 jester
100 buttress
101 cauldron
102 kitchen shed
103 thatch
104 herb bed
105 walled garden
106 fruit tree
107 bellows
108 great oven
109 spit
110 guard
111 firescreen
112 bakehouse
113 packhorse
114 merchant
115 wooden stairs
116 inner bailey
117 stairwell
118 arrow slit
119 smoke hole
120 smithy
121 armorer

122 peasant
123 fish pond
124 laundress
125 shoemaker
126 woodcutter
127 thatcher
128 outer bailey
129 steward
130 nun
131 monk
132 arch
133 logs

134 hounds
135 keeper-of-the-
    hounds
136 cart
137 hut
138 well
139 dovecote
140 doves
141 stable boy
142 perch
143 falconer
144 falcon

145 falcons' mews
146 wall walk
147 curtain wall
148 sentry
149 merlon
150 crenel
151 hoarding
152 gatehouse
153 portcullis
154 drawbridge
155 beggars
156 ditch

21

Music

1 bass drum
2 drumsticks
3 snare drum
4 trombone
5 slide
6 water key
7 kettle drum
8 drumhead
9 foot pedal
10 bassoon
11 crook
12 oboe
13 keys
14 reed
15 flute
16 blow-hole
17 violin
18 chin rest
19 violin bow
20 clarinet
21 viola
22 tailpiece
23 scroll
24 tuba
25 valve
26 mouthpiece
27 French horn
28 cor anglais
29 piccolo
30 lip plate
31 cello
32 orchestra
33 tubular bells
34 xylophone
35 organ
36 stops
37 organ pipes
38 percussion
39 cymbals
40 flautist
41 woodwind
42 brass section
43 string section
44 harpist
45 harp
46 violinists
47 viola players
48 music stand
49 conductor
50 sheet music
51 rostrum
52 cellists
53 double bass
   players
54 rock group
55 speaker
56 drumkit
57 floor tom
58 drummer
59 tom toms
60 crash and ride
   cymbal

61 hihat
62 backup singers
63 microphone
64 reed switch
65 amplifier
66 bass guitarist

67 electric piano
68 moog
   synthesiser
69 lead guitarist
70 electric organ
71 electric guitar

72 headstock
73 neck
74 frets
75 pickup
76 scratchplate
77 tremolo arm

78 controls
79 jack plug socket
80 double bass
   bow
81 double bass
82 strings

111 sleigh bells
112 recorder
113 castanets
114 accordion
115 keyboard
116 harmonica
117 jazz band
118 banjo
119 saxophone
120 jazz singer
121 trumpet
122 trumpeter
123 pianist
124 piano
125 metronome
126 pendulum
127 folk singer
128 Spanish guitar
129 soundhole
130 soundboard
131 concertina
132 brass band
133 drum majorette
134 bugle
135 cornet
136 discothèque
137 disc jockey
138 disco dancers
139 dance floor
140 turntable
141 records
142 steel band
143 steel drum
144 cello pan
145 bass pan
146 ping pongs
147 guitar pan
148 conga drum
149 rhythm section
150 bongo drums
151 tambourine
152 jingles
153 cabasas
154 maracas
155 cow bell
156 claves
157 guiro

83	bridge	90	bagpipes	97	rattle	104	gourd
84	fingerboard	91	melody pipe	98	gong	105	zither
85	tuning pegs	92	windbag	99	vibraphone	106	marimba
86	glockenspiel	93	blowpipe	100	koto	107	balalaika
87	dulcimer	94	drone pipe	101	triangle	108	lute
88	ukelele	95	tenor drones	102	tambura	109	pegbox
89	mandolin	96	wood block	103	sitar	110	handbell

23

In the country

1 otter
2 hedgehog
3 slug
4 shrew
5 stag
6 antlers
7 beetle
8 fawn
9 doe
10 pine cone
11 squirrel
12 drey
13 fox cubs
14 fox
15 badger
16 harvest mouse
17 water vole
18 cloud
19 hang glider
20 hot air balloon
21 gas burner
22 basket
23 sand bag
24 rainbow
25 windmill
26 rain

27 valley
28 backpack
29 piton
30 karabiner
31 climbing
   helmet
32 climbing boot
33 rock climber

34 piton hammer
35 cliff
36 climbing rope
37 climbing
   harness
38 village
39 cemetery
40 kite

41 spire
42 tunnel
43 canal
44 barge
45 church
46 telegraph pole
47 garden shed
48 greenhouse

49 creeper
50 house
51 swing
52 garden
53 plant
54 flower bed
55 lawn
56 sand pit

89 web
90 snail
91 sky
92 hawk
93 hill
94 branch
95 bird
96 nestlings
97 nest
98 quarry
99 power line
100 pylon
101 log cabin
102 lock
103 lake
104 power station
105 hedgerow
106 pony riders
107 tree
108 forest
109 forester
110 hammock
111 tow bar
112 bridge
113 river bank
114 bush
115 camp site
116 barbecue
117 firewood
118 charcoal
119 picnic table
120 camp bed
121 bark
122 angler
123 river
124 compass
125 birdwatcher
126 binoculars
127 map
128 camping stove
129 guy rope
130 water carrier
131 fly sheet
132 torch
133 tent pole
134 ice box
135 air mattress
136 sleeping bag
137 gas lamp
138 tent
139 tent peg
140 moth
141 roots
142 moss
143 tree stump
144 toadstools

57 paddling pool	65 dragonfly	73 tortoise	81 ant	137 gas lamp
58 slide	66 signpost	74 pigeon	82 toad	138 tent
59 climbing frame	67 path	75 ladybird	83 bumblebee	139 tent peg
60 butterfly	68 tackle box	76 pheasant	84 flower	140 moth
61 mole hill	69 fishing rod	77 grasshopper	85 swan	141 roots
62 mole	70 fishing net	78 frog	86 caterpillar	142 moss
63 waterfall	71 grass	79 water lily	87 wasp	143 tree stump
64 hiker	72 swallow	80 lily pad	88 spider	144 toadstools

On the road

1 tandem
2 tricycle
3 scrambler bike
4 racing bike
5 motor scooter
6 moped
7 go-kart
8 bicycle
9 hand grip
10 gear change
   lever
11 handlebar
12 gear cable
13 bell
14 carrier
15 saddle bag
16 saddle
17 seat stem
18 brake lever
19 brake cable
20 horn
21 bicycle lamp
22 bicycle lock
23 rear reflector
24 rear lamp
25 dynamo
26 sprocket
27 chain guard
28 bicycle pump
29 water bottle
   carrier
30 brake calliper
31 mudguard
32 brake block
33 front wheel
34 panniers
35 rear wheel
36 bicycle chain
37 pedal
38 pedal crank
39 kickstand
40 chain wheel
41 frame
42 front fork
43 wheel rim
44 valve
45 spokes
46 spoke reflector
47 inner tube
48 puncture repair
   kit
49 water bottle
50 spanners
51 tire levers
52 motorbike
53 twist throttle
54 clutch lever
55 rearview mirror
56 passenger seat
57 gas tank
58 spark plug
59 carburetor

60 kick start lever
61 rear drum brake
62 front disc brake
63 hydraulic fork
64 rear brake
   pedal
65 foot rest
66 muffler
67 gloves
68 visor
69 crash helmet
70 sports car
71 racing car
72 dragster
73 sidecar
74 dune buggy
75 vintage car
76 land rover
77 van
78 tow truck
79 tank truck
80 moving van
81 camper
82 car transporter
83 coach
84 bus
85 double-decker
   bus
86 trolley bus
87 estate car
88 ambulance
89 fire engine
90 trash hauler

91 semi-truck
92 truck
93 garage
94 gas pump
95 car wash
96 inspection bay
97 roof rack
98 mechanic

99 hydraulic lift
100 air pump
101 car
102 front wing
103 side light
104 front bumper
105 headlamp
106 car radiator

107 fan belt
108 cooling fan
109 cylinder head
110 air filter
111 car battery
112 wing mirror
113 front
    suspension

114 chassis	122 steering wheel	130 gear stick	138 spare wheel	146 gas cap
115 piston	123 dashboard	131 hand brake	139 reversing light	147 wheel hub
116 distributor	124 seat belt	132 back seat	140 foot pump	148 wedge
117 oil filter	125 headrest	133 muffler	141 number plate	149 oil can
118 oil pan	126 accelerator	134 universal joint	142 exhaust pipe	150 tool box
119 speedometer	127 foot brake	135 drive shaft	143 rear bumper	151 lug wrench
120 gas gauge	128 clutch	136 trunk	144 rear light	152 jack
121 windshield	129 gear box	137 brake light	145 indicator light	153 tire

In the city

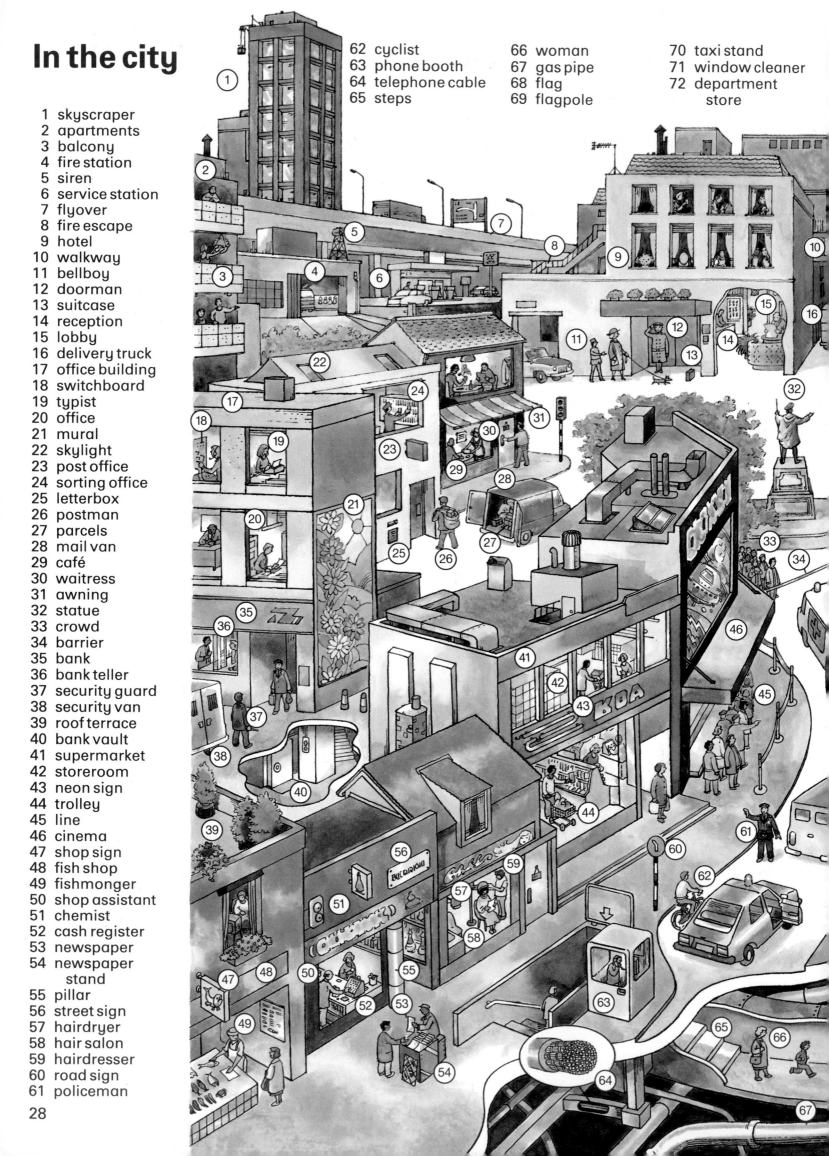

1 skyscraper
2 apartments
3 balcony
4 fire station
5 siren
6 service station
7 flyover
8 fire escape
9 hotel
10 walkway
11 bellboy
12 doorman
13 suitcase
14 reception
15 lobby
16 delivery truck
17 office building
18 switchboard
19 typist
20 office
21 mural
22 skylight
23 post office
24 sorting office
25 letterbox
26 postman
27 parcels
28 mail van
29 café
30 waitress
31 awning
32 statue
33 crowd
34 barrier
35 bank
36 bank teller
37 security guard
38 security van
39 roof terrace
40 bank vault
41 supermarket
42 storeroom
43 neon sign
44 trolley
45 line
46 cinema
47 shop sign
48 fish shop
49 fishmonger
50 shop assistant
51 chemist
52 cash register
53 newspaper
54 newspaper stand
55 pillar
56 street sign
57 hairdryer
58 hair salon
59 hairdresser
60 road sign
61 policeman

62 cyclist
63 phone booth
64 telephone cable
65 steps

66 woman
67 gas pipe
68 flag
69 flagpole

70 taxi stand
71 window cleaner
72 department store

28

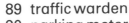

73 street lamp
74 hospital
75 school
76 school teacher

77 school children
78 taxi
79 road sweeper
80 trash cart

81 litter
82 revolving door
83 window dresser
84 dummy

85 porter
86 patient
87 ramp
88 stroller

89 traffic warden
90 parking meter
91 park bench
92 nanny
93 baby buggy
94 fountain
95 park
96 gatepost
97 railings
98 motorcyclist
99 rider
100 bus stop
101 bus driver
102 passengers
103 smoke
104 fireman
105 warning light
106 fire
107 fire hose
108 jumping sheet
109 advertisement
110 bookstall
111 bookseller
112 carrier bag
113 shoe stall
114 shoes
115 souvenir stall
116 tee shirts
117 poster
118 badges
119 fruit stall
120 stretcher
121 accident
122 fire hydrant
123 pavement
124 curb
125 tramp
126 paintings
127 traffic light
128 vegetable stall
129 toy stall
130 clothes stall
131 jersey
132 trousers
133 dresses
134 hats
135 clothes rack
136 socks
137 coats
138 flower seller
139 street map
140 transformer
141 manhole cover
142 litter basket
143 crossing
144 pedestrian
145 manhole
146 electricity cable
147 man
148 underpass
149 water pipe
150 sewage
151 sewer
152 valve box
153 gate key
154 grating

29

Toys and games

1 doll
2 rag doll
3 princess
4 prince
5 king
6 crown
7 queen
8 fairy
9 wand
10 ballerina
11 broomstick
12 witch
13 bride
14 bridegroom
15 bridesmaid
16 page
17 sailor
18 mobile
19 parrot
20 blackboard
21 pencil case
22 fountain pen
23 ballpoint pen
24 pencils
25 wax crayons
26 rubber
27 ruler
28 poster paints
29 felt tip pens
30 numbers
31 letters
32 notebook
33 abacus
34 beads
35 building blocks
36 magnet
37 globe
38 chemistry set
39 test tube
40 spirit burner
41 beaker
42 funnel
43 flask
44 magnifying glass
45 microscope
46 kaleidoscope
47 balloons
48 paper hats
49 fireworks
50 lantern
51 totem pole
52 wigwam
53 head-dress
54 Indian chief
55 squaw
56 papoose
57 fort
58 cavalry man
59 Indian brave
60 tomahawk
61 jack-in-the-box
62 music box

63 money box
64 ferris wheel
65 carousel
66 rocking horse
67 puppet theatre

68 string puppet
69 glove puppet
70 dolls' house
71 cradle
72 polar bear

73 panda
74 rhinoceros
75 camel
76 penguins
77 kangaroo

30

78 zebra
79 leopard
80 monkey
81 crocodile
82 ghost

83 angel
84 wizard
85 pistol
86 pirate
87 treasure

88 monster
89 dragon
90 elf
91 gnome
92 sleigh

93 Santa Claus
94 teddy bear
95 reindeer
96 Christmas
   stocking

97 purse
98 money
99 embroidery
100 wool
101 knitting needle
102 tank
103 infantry men
104 crane
105 excavator
106 remote control
    car
107 race track
108 spaceship
109 hobby horse
110 pogo stick
111 stilts
112 hulahoop
113 scooter
114 skipping rope
115 spinning top
116 bowling pins
117 marbles
118 board game
119 playing cards
120 dice
121 counters
122 chess-board
123 chessmen
124 jigsaw puzzle
125 dominoes
126 puzzle
127 snooker table
128 snooker ball
129 cue
130 robot
131 rattle
132 lunch box
133 penknife
134 key ring
135 keys
136 flashlight
137 typewriter
138 radio
139 record player
140 walkie-talkie
141 cassette
    recorder
142 cassettes
143 electronic
    games
144 cartridge
145 television game
146 handsets
147 computer
148 calculator
149 tiger
150 lion
151 elephant
152 hippopotamus
153 koala bear
154 giraffe
155 ostrich
156 buffalo
157 wolf
158 snake
159 dinosaur

Jobs people do

1 **weaver**
2 dye bath
3 loom
4 woven cloth
5 cloth roller
6 ratchet
7 treadles
8 yarn
9 boat shuttle
10 rug beater
11 bobbin winder
12 **potter**
13 kiln
14 clay
15 modeling tools
16 callipers
17 potter's knife
18 turning tool
19 cutting wire
20 potter's wheel
21 splashpan
22 glaze
23 **blacksmith**
24 fuller
25 flatter
26 stamp
27 scroll iron
28 scroll dog
29 vice
30 fire irons
31 firehood
32 iron
33 water trough
34 tongs
35 swage block
36 horseshoeing
    box
37 mandrel
38 sledge hammer
39 anvil
40 **artist**
41 canvas
42 model
43 canvas
    stretcher
44 paintbox
45 oil paints
46 smock
47 rag
48 easel
49 sketch pad
50 dais
51 stapler
52 palette
53 dipper
54 palette knife
55 brushes
56 painting knife
57 charcoal sticks
58 turpentine
59 **gardener**
60 compost heap

61 trellis
62 plant cover
63 flowerpots
64 cold frame
65 twine
66 dibber

67 gardening
    gloves
68 garden tools
69 wheelbarrow
70 shears
71 lawn mower

72 garden basket
73 seedlings
74 seed tray
75 watering can
76 rose
77 bulbs

78 pruning shears
79 **dressmaker**
80 sewing
    machine
81 cotton reel
82 tension dial

106 mitre block
107 moulding
108 photographer
109 camera
110 wind-on lever
111 shutter button
112 shutter speed control
113 flash shoe
114 rewind lever
115 aperture control
116 focus control
117 lens
118 light screen
119 wind machine
120 film cassette
121 tripod
122 background paper
123 darkroom
124 safelight
125 umbrella light
126 strobe light
127 power unit
128 telephoto lens
129 slide projector
130 flash gun
131 camera case
132 prints
133 cook
134 sieve
135 whisk
136 rolling pin
137 apron
138 piping bag
139 spatula
140 pastry brush
141 cake pan
142 chopping board
143 cook's knife
144 lemon squeezer
145 scales
146 measuring cup
147 food processor
148 wooden spoons
149 mixing bowl
150 grater
151 silversmith
152 silver
153 bench block
154 burnisher
155 propane torch
156 stones
157 bracelets
158 polishing machine
159 jeweler's saw
160 tweezers
161 pliers
162 brooch
163 ring
164 necklace

83 pressure foot	89 sewing box	**95 picture framer**	100 G-cramp
84 bobbin	90 dress pattern	96 hardboard	101 hand drill
85 tape measure	91 buttons	97 picture glass	102 mitre cramp
86 scissors	92 pins	98 mounting board	103 claw hammer
87 needles	93 pin cushion	99 metal ruler	104 craft knife
88 material	94 thread		105 tenon saw

On the rails

1 **marshalling yard**
2 freight train
3 freight car
4 scanner
5 container
6 grab
7 gantry crane
8 boxcar
9 lighting tower
10 open goods wagon
11 signal box
12 signalman
13 tank car
14 warehouse
15 flat car
16 loading foreman
17 weighing machine
18 crates
19 switch signal
20 signals
21 switch engine
22 **station**
23 station clock
24 loudspeaker
25 left luggage office
26 ticket office
27 information office
28 newsagent
29 magazines
30 water fountain
31 underground entrance
32 thief
33 handbag
34 platform number
35 walking-stick
36 electric truck
37 ticket machine
38 turnstile
39 fire extinguisher
40 lift
41 emergency button
42 landing
43 escalator
44 emergency stairs
45 street musician
46 ventilation shaft
47 steel girder
48 fan
49 underground train map
50 exit sign

51 vending machine
52 electric rail
53 underground train
54 platform
55 mailbags
56 buffer
57 railway track
58 **electric locomotive**
59 engineer
60 insulator
61 roof cable
62 oil cooler
63 battery box
64 electric motor
65 pantograph
66 overhead wire
67 windshield wiper

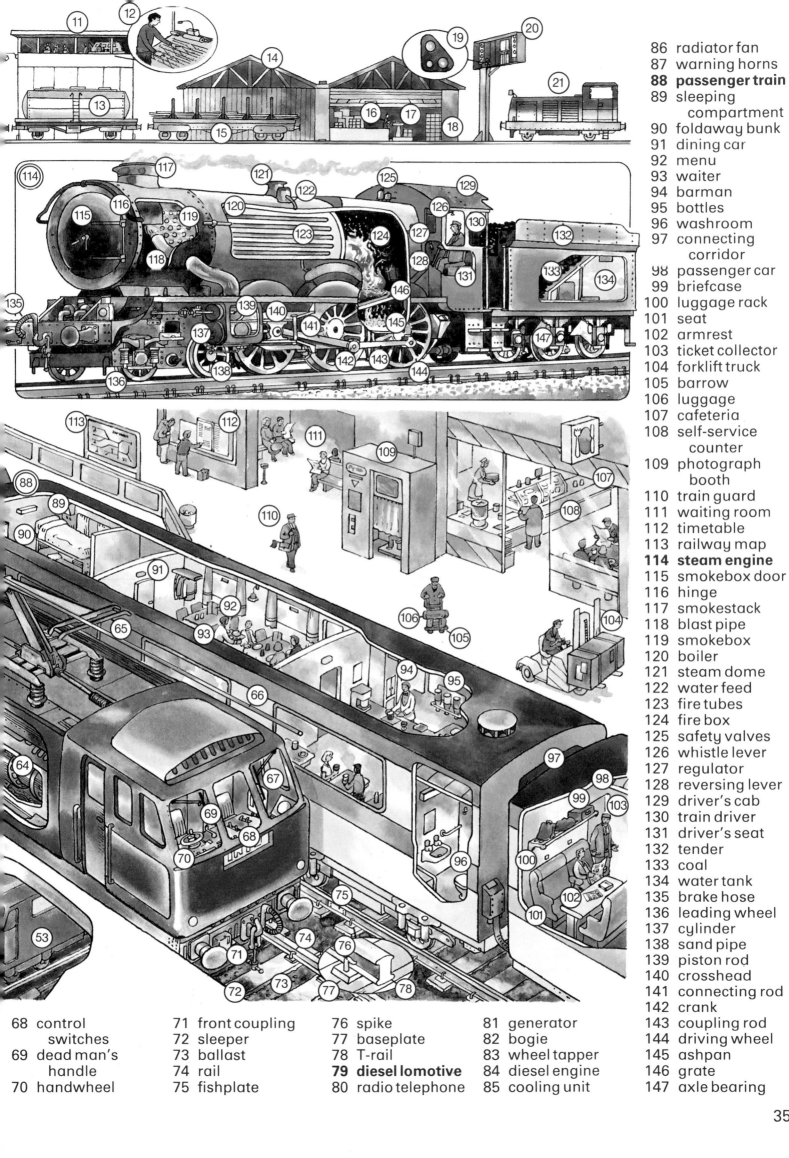

86 radiator fan
87 warning horns
88 passenger train
89 sleeping compartment
90 foldaway bunk
91 dining car
92 menu
93 waiter
94 barman
95 bottles
96 washroom
97 connecting corridor
98 passenger car
99 briefcase
100 luggage rack
101 seat
102 armrest
103 ticket collector
104 forklift truck
105 barrow
106 luggage
107 cafeteria
108 self-service counter
109 photograph booth
110 train guard
111 waiting room
112 timetable
113 railway map
114 steam engine
115 smokebox door
116 hinge
117 smokestack
118 blast pipe
119 smokebox
120 boiler
121 steam dome
122 water feed
123 fire tubes
124 fire box
125 safety valves
126 whistle lever
127 regulator
128 reversing lever
129 driver's cab
130 train driver
131 driver's seat
132 tender
133 coal
134 water tank
135 brake hose
136 leading wheel
137 cylinder
138 sand pipe
139 piston rod
140 crosshead
141 connecting rod
142 crank
143 coupling rod
144 driving wheel
145 ashpan
146 grate
147 axle bearing

68 control switches
69 dead man's handle
70 handwheel
71 front coupling
72 sleeper
73 ballast
74 rail
75 fishplate
76 spike
77 baseplate
78 T-rail
79 diesel lomotive
80 radio telephone
81 generator
82 bogie
83 wheel tapper
84 diesel engine
85 cooling unit

In the studio

1 actress
2 actor
3 producer
4 script
5 writer
6 casting director
7 clipboard
8 filing cabinet
9 tape recorder
10 paint trolley
11 scenic artist
12 scenery
13 backdrop
14 floor plan
15 desk lamp
16 set designer
17 scenery builder
18 drawing board
19 set model
20 prop store
21 skeleton
22 prop master
23 crutch
24 masks
25 wheelchair
26 throne
27 artificial plant
28 trophy
29 gramophone
30 costume room
31 caps
32 bonnet
33 cloak
34 top hat
35 shawl
36 veil
37 coat hanger
38 tutu
39 historical
    costume
40 bouquet
41 costume
    designer
42 wedding dress
43 belt
44 raincoat
45 sleeve
46 collar
47 medals
48 uniform
49 ties
50 blouses
51 spectacles
52 wigs
53 mirror lights
54 stethoscope
55 waistcoat
56 make-up artist
57 hair curlers
58 moustaches
59 scar
60 blow dryer

61 cotton balls
62 modeling clay
63 false beard
64 false nose
65 grease paint

66 false teeth
67 make-up box
68 lipstick
69 face powder
70 powder puff

71 headphones
72 teleprompt
    operator
73 teleprompt
74 weather reporter

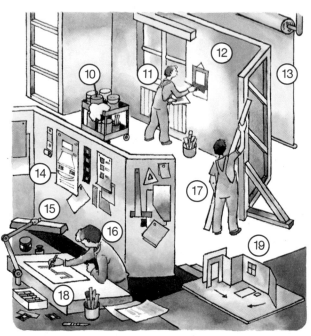

36

75 weather chart	80 newscaster
76 caption roller	**81 studio**
77 digital clock	82 overhead light
78 desk	83 spotlight
79 earpiece	84 scarf

85 cleaner	90 nurse
86 mop	91 syringe
87 curtain screen	92 thermometer
88 dressing gown	93 doctor
89 medicine bottle	94 calendar

95 i.v. drip
96 plaster cast
97 present
98 visitor
99 weight
100 scene shifter
101 call boy
102 bandage
103 sticking plaster
104 pills
105 boom operator
106 boom
107 microphone
108 temperature chart
109 studio camera
110 sound technician
111 cameraman
112 floor manager
113 video tape
   recorder
114 studio monitor
115 crane camera
116 zoom lens
117 cue card
118 viewfinder
119 focusing handle
120 pedestal
121 camera cable
**122 sound control
   room**
123 sound
   supervisor
124 sound engineer
**125 production
   control room**
126 video mixer
127 director
128 monitor screen
129 stop watch
130 production
   assistant
131 technical
   manager
**132 video control
   room**
133 video controler
134 lighting director
135 film camera
136 clapperboard
137 stetson
138 sheriff
139 holster
140 spurs
141 chaps
142 bullets
143 handcuffs
144 gun
145 lasso
146 film set
147 sound recordist
148 cowboy
149 bandit
150 stagecoach
151 stuntman
152 money bag
153 airbag

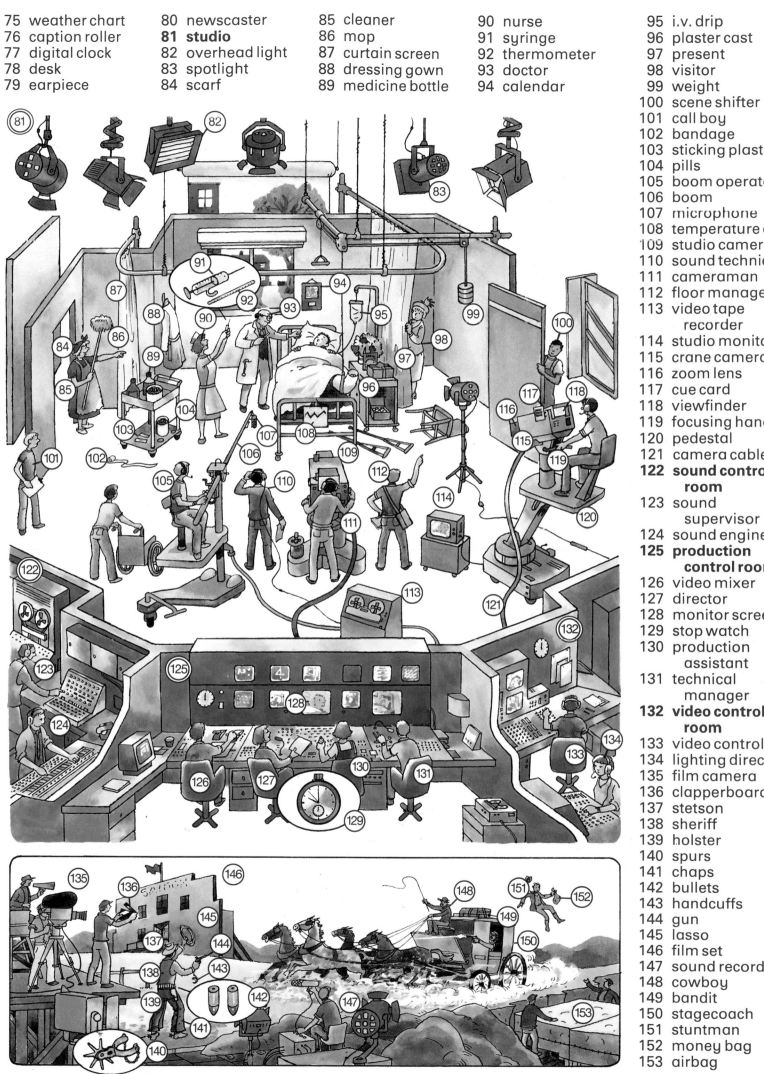

37

On the water

1 **ocean liner**
2 lido
3 sports deck
4 florist's
5 shopping arcade
6 sun deck
7 exhaust stack
8 smoke deflector
9 nightclub
10 lookout tower
11 navigation bridge and chartroom
12 crew's quarters
13 car lift
14 cabins
15 single berth cabin
16 staterooms
17 cocktail lounge
18 library
19 theater and lecture hall
20 casino
21 beauty salon
22 laundry room
23 ballroom
24 wine cellar
25 restaurant
26 children's playroom
27 portholes
28 bow thrusters
29 hawsehole
30 **hovercraft**
31 control deck
32 car ramp

71 flare
72 sextant
73 life buoy
74 batten
75 sail bag
76 anemometer
77 barometer
78 chart
79 paddle
80 fender
81 pennant
82 bailer
83 launching trolley
84 **cargo ship**
85 poop deck
86 davit
87 lifeboats
88 funnel
89 fog horn
90 wheelhouse
91 cross-trees
92 crow's nest
93 foredeck
94 derrick
95 forecastle
96 windlass
97 jack
98 jackstaff
99 hull
100 propeller shaft
101 turbines
102 engine room
103 anchor cable
104 **tanker**
105 fire tower
106 mooring winch
107 kingpost
108 cargo tanks
109 **rescue launch**
110 guard rail
111 inflatable liferaft
112 towing davit

33 flexible skirt
34 passenger
   steps
35 hydrofoil
36 motor boat
37 deckhouse
38 outboard motor
39 steering arm

40 powerboat
41 fireboat
42 hosereels
43 scuppers
44 police launch
45 lightship
46 lantern mast
47 tug

48 bow fender
49 pilot house
50 searchlight
51 towing lights
52 tow hook
53 capstan
54 trawler
55 trawl gallows

56 trawl net
57 bucket dredger
58 bucket chain
59 chute
60 sloop
61 spinnaker
62 spinnaker
   boom

63 catamaran
64 trimaran
65 outrigger
66 schooner
67 foresail
68 racing yacht
69 genoa
70 keel

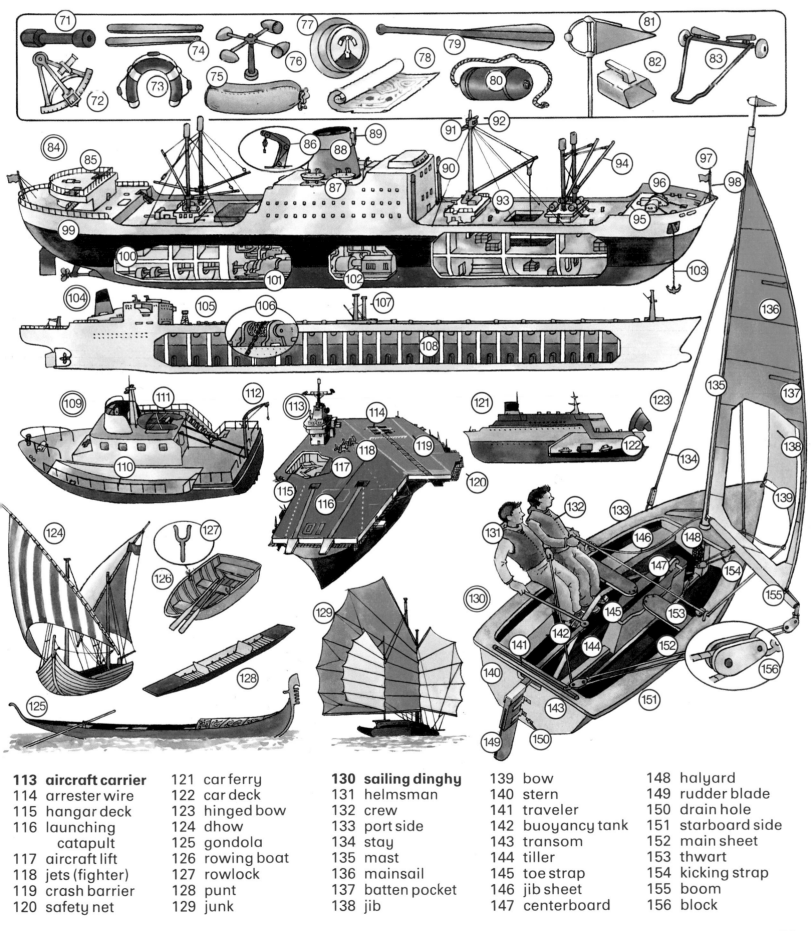

113 aircraft carrier
114 arrester wire
115 hangar deck
116 launching
   catapult
117 aircraft lift
118 jets (fighter)
119 crash barrier
120 safety net

121 car ferry
122 car deck
123 hinged bow
124 dhow
125 gondola
126 rowing boat
127 rowlock
128 punt
129 junk

130 sailing dinghy
131 helmsman
132 crew
133 port side
134 stay
135 mast
136 mainsail
137 batten pocket
138 jib

139 bow
140 stern
141 traveler
142 buoyancy tank
143 transom
144 tiller
145 toe strap
146 jib sheet
147 centerboard

148 halyard
149 rudder blade
150 drain hole
151 starboard side
152 main sheet
153 thwart
154 kicking strap
155 boom
156 block

In space

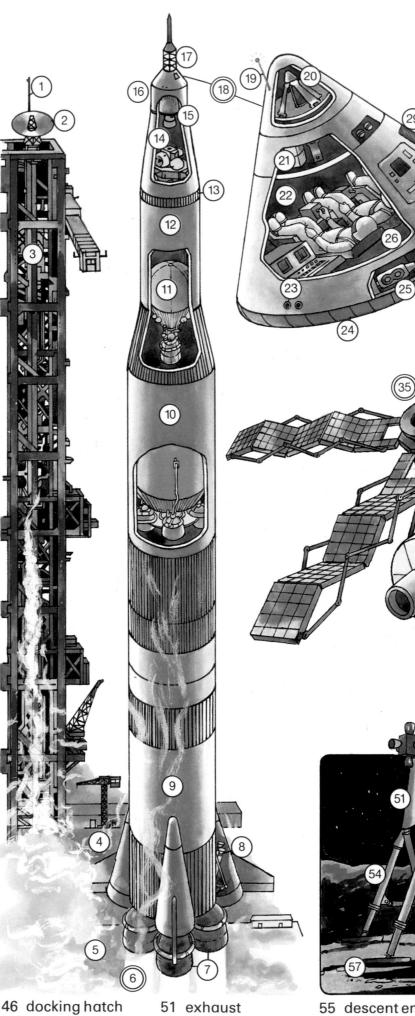

1 lightning rod
2 radio telescope
3 gantry
4 space launch station
5 launch pad
6 space rocket
7 rocket engines
8 retro-rockets
9 first stage
10 second stage
11 liquid oxygen tank
12 third stage
13 instrument unit
14 lunar module hangar
15 engine nozzle
16 service module
17 launch escape tower
18 command module
19 recovery beacon
20 docking probe
21 main recovery parachute
22 crew compartment
23 yaw thrusters
24 heatshield
25 roll thrusters
26 padded couch
27 pitch thrusters
28 hatch door
29 rendezvous window
30 weather satellite
31 communications satellite
32 earth resources satellite
33 space probe
34 cosmic ray detector
35 space station
36 solar shield
37 solar panel
38 micrometeoroid shield
39 orbital workshop
40 sleep compartment
41 exercise bicycle
42 solar wing
43 deployment boom
44 docking port
45 lunar module

46 docking hatch
47 rendezvous radar antenna
48 inflight antenna
49 tracking light
50 entry hatch
51 exhaust deflector
52 ascent engine
53 entry/exit platform
54 landing gear

55 descent engine
56 thermal insulation
57 foot pad
58 moon rock
59 lunar surface

60 lunar rover
61 high-gain antenna
62 low-gain antenna
63 camera pack
64 display console

40

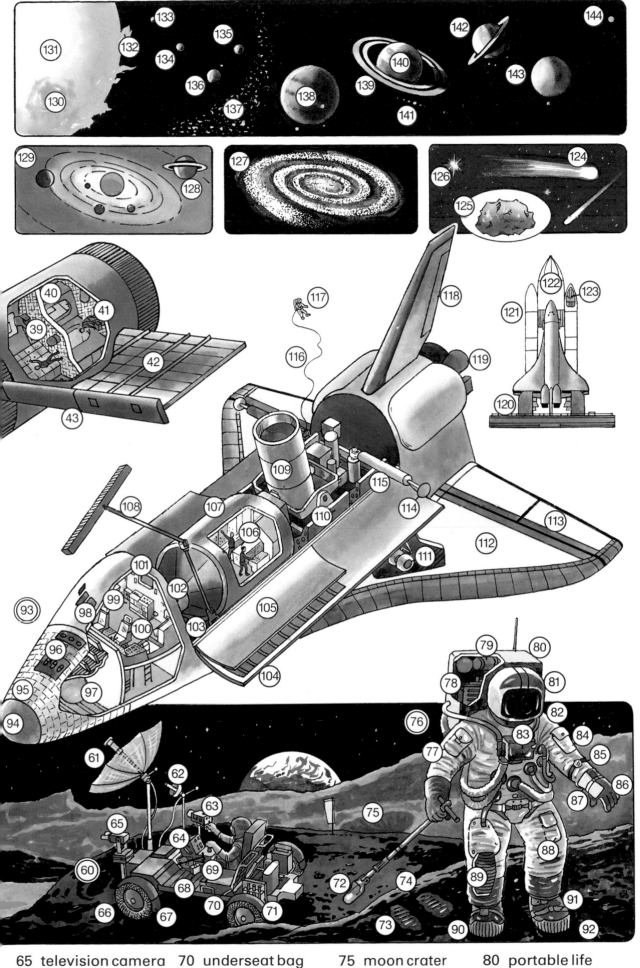

84 penlight pocket
85 chronograph
86 extra-vehicular glove
87 checklist
88 utility pocket
89 rubber innersuit
90 lunar overshoe
91 clip
92 moonwalk
93 space shuttle
94 nose cap
95 heat insulation tiles
96 rocket thrusters
97 oxidizer tank
98 pilot's seat
99 docking controls
100 commander's seat
101 rearview window
102 access tunnel
103 payload bay
104 payload bay door
105 space radiator
106 payload specialists
107 space laboratory
108 robot arm
109 space telescope
110 pallet
111 main wheels
112 delta wing
113 elevon
114 magnetometer
115 sensor
116 umbilical line
117 spacewalk
118 speed brake
119 maneuvering engine
120 launch support
121 solid rocket booster
122 external tank
123 drogue parachute
124 comet
125 meteorite
126 star
127 Milky Way
128 planet
129 solar system
130 sunspot
131 Sun
132 solar flare
133 Mercury
134 Venus
135 Mars
136 Earth
137 asteroids
138 Jupiter
139 Saturn's rings
140 Saturn
141 Moon
142 Uranus
143 Neptune
144 Pluto

65 television camera
66 wiremesh wheel
67 dust guard
68 sample bag dispenser
69 rock tongs
70 underseat bag stowage
71 tool carrier
72 scoop
73 footprint
74 moon dust
75 moon crater
76 astronaut
77 sunglasses pocket
78 transceiver
79 airtank
80 portable life support system
81 pressurized helmet
82 spacesuit
83 control box

Index

This is a list of all the words in the pictures. They are in alphabetical order. After each word there are two numbers. The first tells you what number the object is on the page, the second tells you which page to find it on.

abacus **33**, p.30
accelerator **126**, p.27
access tunnel **102**, p.41
accident **121**, p.29
accordion **114**, p.23
acoustic probe **146**, p.17
actor **2**, p.36
actress **1**, p.36
adjustable spanner **79**, p.4
advertisement **109**, p.29
aileron **17**, p.14
airbag **153**, p.37
airbrake **30**, p.15
air conditioning vehicle **127**, p.14
aircraft carrier 113, p.39
aircraft lift **117**, p.39
air extractor **115**, p.5
air filter **110**, p.27
airline ticket **106**, p.14
air mattress **135**, p.25
air pump **100**, p.27
airport 48, p.14
airport police car **88**, p.15
airport vehicles 124, p.15
airship 34, p.15
airspeed indicator **3**, p.14
airtank **79**, p.41
alarm clock **21**, p.6
alfalfa **24**, p.12
altimeter **4**, p.14
ambulance **88**, p.27
American football 15, p.10
amplifier **65**, p.22
anchor **105**, p.17
anchor cable **103**, p.39
anemometer **76**, p.39
angel **83**, p.31
angler **122**, p.25
ankle bandage **131**, p.11
ant **81**, p.25
antenna **74**, p.15
anti-collision light **81**, p.15
antlers **6**, p.24
anvil **39**, p.32
apartments, **2**, p.28

aperture control **115**, p.33
apples **49**, p.18
apricots **57**, p.18
apron **137**, p.33
aqualung **135**, p.17
arch **132**, p.21
archer **22**, p.21
archery 115, p.11
architect **5**, p.4
arena **7**, p.8
armband **29**, p.16
arm bracer **119**, p.11
armchair **114**, p.7
armorer **121**, p.21
armrest **102**, p.35
arrester wire **114**, p.39
arrivals hall **117**, p.15
arrows **10**, p.20
arrow slit **118**, p.21
artichokes **22**, p.18
artificial horizon **2**, p.14
artificial plant **27**, p.36
artist 40, p.32
ascent engine **52**, p.40
ashpan **145**, p.35
ashtray **116**, p.7
asparagus **23**, p.18
asteroids **137**, p.41
astronaut 76, p.41
asymmetric bars **82**, p.9
athlete **4**, p.8
attic 3, p.6
avocados **35**, p.18
awl **143**, p.5
awning **31**, p.28
axe **12**, p.21
axle bearing **147**, p.35

baby buggy **93**, p.29
backboard **137**, p.11
backdrop **13**, p.36
background paper **122**, p.33
backpack **28**, p.24
back seat **132**, p.27
backstroke **148**, p.9
backup singers **62**, p.22
bacon **111**, p.19
badger **15**, p.24
badges **118**, p.29
badminton 144, p.11
badminton racket **145**, p.11
baggage train **129**, p.14
bagpipes **90**, p.23
baguette **108**, p.11
bailer **82**, p.39
baked beans **164**, p.19

bakehouse **112**, p.21
balalaika **107**, p.23
balcony **3**, p.28
ball and chain **94**, p.20
ballast **73**, p.35
ballast tank **129**, p.17
ball boy **130**, p.9
ballerina **10**, p.30
ballista **18**, p.21
balloons **47**, p.30
ballpoint pen **23**, p.30
balloon **23**, p.38
ballroom **23**, p.38
bananas **39**, p.18
bandage **102**, p.37
bandit **149**, p.37
banisters **35**, p.4
banjo **118**, p.23
bank **35**, p.28
bank teller **36**, p.28
bank vault **40**, p.28
barbecue **116**, p.25
barbell **34**, p.8
barge **44**, p.24
bark **121**, p.25
barley **14**, p.12
barman **94**, p.35
barn **105**, p.13
barnacle **45**, p.16
barn owl **117**, p.13
barometer **77**, p.39
baron **74**, p.20
baroness **76**, p.20
barrel **91**, p.20
barrier **34**, p.28
barrow **105**, p.35
base **48**, p.10
baseball 41, p.10
baseball bat **43**, p.10
baseline **124**, p.9
baseplate **77**, p.35
basil **102**, p.19
basinet **44**, p.20
basket **22**, p.24
basketball 136, p.11
basket rim **138**, p.11
bass drum **1**, p.22
bass guitarist **66**, p.22
bassoon **10**, p.22
bass pan **145**, p.23
bath **43**, p.6
bathing cap **150**, p.9
bathmat **45**, p.6
bathroom 33, p.6
bathroom scales **44**, p.6
bath salts **122**, p.6
bathyscaphe **144**, p.17
baton **32**, p.8
batsman **26**, p.10
batten **18**, p.4
batten (sail) **74**, p.39
batten pocket **137**, p.39

batter **44**, p.10
battering ram **17**, p.21
battery box **63**, p.34
batting glove **34**, p.10
battlements **70**, p.21
bay **88**, p.17
beach bag **23**, p.16
beachball **28**, p.16
beach café **2**, p.16
beach towel **25**, p.16
beads **34**, p.30
beak **91**, p.13
beaker **41**, p.30
beam **81**, p.9
beans **16**, p.18
beans (dried) **139**, p.19
beauty salon **21**, p.38
bed **30**, p.6
bedroom 12, p.6
bedside table **27**, p.6
beehive **43**, p.12
beer **141**, p.19
bees **42**, p.12
beetle **7**, p.24
beetroot **24**, p.18
beggars **155**, p.21
bell **13**, p.26
bellboy **11**, p.28
bellows **107**, p.21
belt **43**, p.36
bench (in castle) **97**, p.21
bench **97**, p.21
bench block **153**, p.33
bicycle 8, p.26
bicycle chain **36**, p.26
bicycle lamp **21**, p.26
bicycle lock **22**, p.26
bicycle pump **28**, p.26
bill **2**, p.20
billy goat **79**, p.13
binoculars **126**, p.25
bird **95**, p.25
bird cage **68**, p.6
bird table **62**, p.12
birdwatcher **125**, p.25
black belt **49**, p.8
blackberries **65**, p.18
blackboard **20**, p.30
blacksmith 23, p.32
blade **10**, p.12
blanket **28**, p.6
blast pipe **118**, p.35
blender **141**, p.6
blind **72**, p.6
blinker **63**, p.10
block **156**, p.39
blouses **50**, p.36
blow dryer **60**, p.36
blow-hole **16**, p.22
blow lamp **82**, p.4
blowpipe **93**, p.23
blueberries **60**, p.18

boar **34**, p.12
board game **118**, p.31
boarding pass **107**, p.14
boat house **152**, p.11
boat shuttle **9** p.32
bobbin **84**, p.33
bobbin winder **11**, p.32
bobsleigh racing 80, p.11
bogie **82**, p.34
boiler **120**, p.35
boiling oil **25**, p.21
bollard **10**, p.18
bolster chisel **66**, p.4
bone **65**, p.6
bongo drums **150**, p.23
bonnet **32**, p.36
bookcase **104**, p.7
bookseller **111**, p.29
bookstall **110**, p.29
boom **106**, p.37
boom **155**, p.39
boom operator **105**, p.37
boost gauge **6**, p.14
boots **60**, p.12
bottles **95**, p.35
boule **107**, p.11
boules 106, p.11
bouquet **40**, p.36
bow **139**, p.39
bow (archery) **117**, p.11
bow fender **48**, p.38
bowl **95**, p.11
bowler **30**, p.10
bowling crease **32**, p.10
bowling green **94**, p.11
bowling mat **93**, p.11
bowling pins **116**, p.31
bowls 92, p.11
bowman **67**, p.10
bowstring **116**, p.11
bow thrusters **28**, p.38
boxcar **8**, p.34
boxer **53**, p.8
boxes **4**, p.6
boxing 51, p.8
boxing ring **55**, p.8
brace and bit **149**, p.5
bracelets **157**, p.33
brake block **32**, p.26
brake cable **19**, p.26
brake calliper **30**, p.26
brake hose **135**, p.35
brake lever **18**, p.26
brake light **137**, p.27
brakeman **82**, p.11
branch **94**, p.25
brass band 132, p.23
brass section **42**, p.22
bread board **89**, p.6
bread rolls **129**, p.19
breadsticks **132**, p.19
breakwater **95**, p.17

breast plate **45**, p.20
breech **27**, p.21
breeches **71**, p.8
breeze block **54**, p.4
brick hammer **71**, p.4
bricklayer **62**, p.4
bricks **48**, p.4
bride **13**, p.30
bridegroom **14**, p.30
bridesmaid **15**, p.30
bridge **112**, p.25
bridge (on double bass) **83**, p.23
briefcase **99**, p.35
broadsword **52**, p.20
broccoli **13**, p.18
brooch **162**, p.33
broom **59**, p.12
broomstick **11**, p.30
brown bread **126**, p.19
brushes **55**, p.32
Brussels sprouts **11**, p.18
buck **85**, p.9
bucket **32**, p.16
bucket chain **58**, p.38
bucket dredger **57**, p.38
buffalo **156**, p.31
buffer **56**, p.34
bugle **134**, p.23
building blocks **35**, p.30
bulb (light) **10**, p.6
bulbs (garden) **77**, p.32
bulkhead **70**, p.15
bull **29**, p.12
bulldozer **1**, p.4
bullets **142**, p.37
bull's eye **121**, p.11
bumblebee **83**, p.25
bunkbeds **57**, p.7
bunker **112**, p.9
buoy **98**, p.17
buoyancy tank **142**, p.39
burglar alarm **92**, p.5
burnisher **154**, p.33
bus **84**, p.27
bus driver **101**, p.29
bush **114**, p.25
bus stop **100**, p.29
butter **166**, p.19
butter dish **138**, p.6
butterfly **60**, p.24
buttons **91**, p.33
buttress **100**, p.21

cabasas **153**, p.23
cabbage **17**, p.18

cabins **14**, p.38
cable **131**, p.17
cable car **4**, p.10
caddie **106**, p.9
café **29**, p.28
cafeteria **107**, p.35
cage **130**, p.17
cake **134**, p.19
cake pan **141**, p.33
calculator **148**, p.31
calendar **94**, p.37
calf **27**, p.12
call boy **101**, p.37
callipers **16**, p.32
camel **75**, p.30
camera 109, p.33
camera cable **121**, p.37
camera case **131**, p.33
cameraman **111**, p.37
camera pack **63**, p.41
camp bed **120**, p.25
camper **81**, p.27
camping stove **128**, p.25
camp site **115**, p.25
canal **43**, p.24
candies **162**, p.19
candle **87**, p.21
candlestick **156**, p.7
cannon 26, p.21
cannon balls **30**, p.21
canoeing 65, p.10
can opener **140**, p.6
canvas **41**, p.32
canvas stretcher **43**, p.32
caps **31**, p.36
capstan **53**, p.38
captain **83**, p.11
caption roller **76**, p.36
car 101, p.27
car battery **111**, p.27
carburetor **59**, p.26
car deck **122**, p.39
car ferry **121**, p.39
cargo container **58**, p.14
cargo hold **67**, p.14
cargo ship 84, p.39
cargo tanks **108**, p.39
car lift **13**, p.38
carousel **65**, p.30
car park **49**, p.14
car rental **116**, p.15
carpenter **136**, p.5
carpet layer **93**, p.5
car radiator **106**, p.27
car ramp **32**, p.38
carrier **14**, p.26
carrier bag **112**, p.29
carrots **4**, p.18
cart **136**, p.21
carthorse **85**, p.13
car transporter **82**, p.27
cartridge **144**, p.31

cartridges (rifle) **104**, p.11
carving fork **147**, p.7
carving knife **146**, p.7
car wash **95**, p.27
cash register **52**, p.28
casino **20**, p.38
casserole dish **152**, p.7
cassette recorder **141**, p.31
cassettes **142**, p.31
castanets **113**, p.23
casting director **6**, p.36
castle 68, p.20
cat **56**, p.12
catamaran **63**, p.38
catcher **42**, p.10
caterpillar **86**, p.25
cat flap **64**, p.6
cattle grid **104**, p.13
cauldron **101**, p.21
cauliflower **14**, p.18
cavalry man **58**, p.30
cave **1**, p.16
caviar **85**, p.18
cavity wall **43**, p.4
ceiling **101**, p.5
ceiling joist **53**, p.4
celery **15**, p.18
cellist **52**, p.22
cello, **31**, p.22
cello pan **144**, p.23
cement **29**, p.4
cement mixer **28**, p.4
cemetery **39**, p.24
centerboard **147**, p.39
center line **99**, p.11
cereal **159**, p.19
cesta (basket) **133**, p.11
cinema **46**, p.28
cinema screen **73**, p.15
chain guard **27**, p.26
chain mail **41**, p.20
chain wheel **40**, p.26
chair **94**, p.6
chair lift **5**, p.10
changing room **6**, p.16
chapel **81**, p.21
chaplain **79**, p.21
chaps **141**, p.37
charcoal **118**, p.25
charcoal sticks **57**, p.32
chart **78**, p.39
chassis **114**, p.27
check-in desk **111**, p.14
checklist **87**, p.41
cheese **165**, p.19
cheesecake **95**, p.18
chemist **51**, p.28
chemistry set **38**, p.30
cherry picker **131**, p.14
chess-board **122**, p.31
chessman **123**, p.31
chest-of-drawers **32**, p.6

chicory **29**, p.18
children's playroom **26**, p.38
chimes **62**, p.6
chimney pot **24**, p.4
chimney stack **23**, p.4
chin rest **18**, p.22
chipboard **46**, p.4
chisel **141**, p.5
chives **103**, p.19
chocolate sauce **88**, p.18
chopping board **142**, p.33
chops **112**, p.19
Christmas stocking **96**, p.31
chronograph **85**, p.41
church **45**, p.24
chute **59**, p.38
clapperboard **136**, p.37
clarinet **20**, p.22
claves **156**, p.23
claw **40**, p.16
claw hammer **103**, p.33
clay **14**, p.32
cleaner **85**, p.37
cliff **35**, p.24
climbing boot **32**, p.24
climbing frame **59**, p.24
climbing harness **37**, p.24
climbing helmet **31**, p.24
climbing rope **36**, p.24
clip **91**, p.41
clipboard **7**, p.36
clips (for croquet) **123**, p.11
cloak **33**, p.36
clothes rack **135**, p.29
clothes stall **130**, p.29
cloth roller **5**, p.32
cloud **18**, p.24
clover **23**, p.12
club hammer **67**, p.4
club house **114**, p.9
clutch **128**, p.27
clutch lever **54**, p.26
coach **83**, p.27
coach (trainer) **9**, p.8
coal **133**, p.35
coast guard **82**, p.17
coat hanger **37**, p.36
coat-of-arms **50**, p.20
coat rack **99**, p.7
coats **137**, p.29
cob **20**, p.12
cockerel **89**, p.13
cockles **48**, p.16
cockpit cover **16**, p.14
cocktail lounge **17**, p.38
coconuts **38**, p.18
coffee **143**, p.19
coffee beans **144**, p.19
coffee pot **135**, p.6
coffee table **115**, p.7

colander **157**, p.7
cold frame **64**, p.32
cold water pipe **104**, p.5
cold water tank **103**, p.5
collar **46**, p.36
comb **125**, p.6
combine harvester **139**, p.13
comet **124**, p.41
comforter **26**, p.6
command module 18, p.40
commander's seat **100**, p.41
communications satellite **31**, p.40
compass **124**, p.25
competitors **12**, p.8
compost heap **60**, p.32
computer **147**, p.31
concertina **131**, p.23
concrete **134**, p.5
conductor **49**, p.22
conga drum **148**, p.23
connecting corridor **97**, p.35
connecting rod **141**, p.35
conning tower **127**, p.17
container **5**, p.34
contestant **38**, p.8
control box **83**, p.41
control deck **31**, p.38
controls **78**, p.22
control stick **10**, p.14
control switches **68**, p.35
control tower **53**, p.14
conveyor belt **110**, p.14
cook 133, p.33
cookies **135**, p.19
cook's knife **143**, p.33
cooling fan **108**, p.27
cooling unit **85**, p.34
co-pilot **85**, p.15
coral **125**, p.17
cor anglais **28**, p.22
corkscrew **148**, p.7
cormorant **20**, p.16
corn **109**, p.13
corner cushion **56**, p.8
corner flag **20**, p.10
cornet **135**, p.23
cornice **83**, p.5
coronel **61**, p.20
cosmic ray detector **34**, p.40
costume designer **41**, p.36
costume room 30, p.36
cot **5**, p.6
cotton balls **61**, p.36
cotton reel **81**, p.33
counters **121**, p.31
coupling rod **143**, p.35

cow **25**, p.12
cow bell **155**, p.23
cowboy **148**, p.37
cowshed **111**, p.13
cox **149**, p.11
crab **41**, p.16
crab pot **106**, p.17
cradle **71**, p.30
craft knife **104**, p.33
cranberries **64**, p.18
crane **104**, p.31
crane camera **115**, p.37
crank **142**, p.35
crash and ride cymbals **60**, p.22
crash barrier **119**, p.39
crash helmet **69**, p.26
crates **18**, p.35
cream **149**, p.19
creeper **49**, p.24
crenel **150**, p.21
crest **65**, p.20
crew **132**, p.39
crew bus **134**, p.15
crew compartment **22**, p.40
crew's quarters **12**, p.38
cricket 24, p.10
cricket ball **31**, p.10
cricket bat **27**, p.10
cricket pad **29**, p.10
crocodile **81**, p.30
croissants **128**, p.19
crook **11**, p.22
crops 11, p.12
croquet 122, p.11
croquet ball **126**, p.11
croquet mallet **124**, p.11
cross **80**, p.21
crossbar **21**, p.8
crossbow **5**, p.20
crosse **40**, p.10
crosshead **140**, p.35
crossing **143**, p.29
cross-trees **91**, p.39
crowd **33**, p.28
crown **6**, p.30
crow's nest **92**, p.39
crutch **23**, p.36
cucumber **31**, p.18
cue **129**, p.31
cue card **117**, p.37
cuff **74**, p.8
cultivator **142**, p.13
cup **123**, p.6
curb **124**, p.29
curling 86, p.11
curling broom **87**, p.11
curling stone **91**, p.11
curtain **18**, p.6
curtain rail **13**, p.6
curtain screen **87**, p.37

curtain wall **147**, p.21
cushion **31**, p.6
custard **96**, p.18
customs control **118**, p.15
cutting wire **19**, p.32
cuttlefish **75**, p.16
cuttlefish bone **30**, p.16
cyclist **62**, p.28
cylinder **137**, p.35
cylinder head **109**, p.27
cymbals **39**, p.22

Dd

dagger **15**, p.21
dairy **123**, p.13
dairyman **133**, p.13
dais **50**, p.32
damp proof course **60**, p.4
dance floor **139**, p.23
darkroom **123**, p.33
dart **40**, p.8
dartboard **44**, p.8
darts player **41**, p.8
dashboard **123**, p.27
dates **56**, p.18
daughter **55**, p.7
davit **86**, p.39
dead man's handle **69**, p.35
deck (on kayak) **68**, p.10
deckchair **26**, p.16
deckhouse **37**, p.38
deep sea diver **141**, p.17
delivery truck **16**, p.28
delta wing **112**, p.41
department store **72**, p.29
departure gate **102**, p.14
departure hall **112**, p.14
departure lounge **104**, p.14
deployment boom **43**, p.41
depth gauge **138**, p.17
derrick **94**, p.39
descent engine **55**, p.40
desk **78**, p.36
desk lamp **15**, p.36
detergent **136**, p.6
dhow **124**, p.39
dibber **66**, p.32
dice **120**, p.31
diesel engine **84**, p.34
diesel locomotive 79, p.34
digging fork **3**, p.12
digital clock **77**, p.36
dining car **91**, p.35
dinosaur **159**, p.31
dipper **53**, p.32
director **127**, p.37

disc jockey **137**, p.23
disco dancers **138**, p.23
discothèque 136, p.23
discs **33**, p.8
discus thrower **27**, p.8
dishwasher **76**, p.6
display console **64**, p.41
distributor **116**, p.27
ditch **156**, p.21
diver **144**, p.9
diving-board **146**, p.9
diving helmet **142**, p.1/
diving saucer **76**, p.16
docking controls **99**, p.41
docking hatch **46**, p.40
docking port **44**, p.41
docking probe **20**, p.40
doctor **93**, p.37
doe **9**, p.24
dog basket **95**, p.6
dog bowl **66**, p.6
doll **1**, p.30
dolls' house **70**, p.30
dolphin **63**, p.16
dominoes **125**, p.31
donkey **82**, p.13
door **49**, p.6
door bell **63**, p.6
door frame **99**, p.5
doorman **12**, p.28
doormat **102**, p.7
double bass **81**, p.23
double bass bow **80**, p.23
double bass players **53**, p.22
double-decker bus **85**, p.27
doubles sideline **126**, p.9
doughnuts **131**, p.19
dovecote **139**, p.21
doves **140**, p.21
dragon **89**, p.31
dragonfly **65**, p.24
dragster **72**, p.27
drain hole **150**, p.39
draining board **73**, p.6
drainpipe **119**, p.5
drawbridge **154**, p.21
drawing board **18**, p.36
dresser **81**, p.6
dresses **133**, p.29
dressing gown **88**, p.37
dressing table **22**, p.6
dressmaker 79, p.33
dress pattern **90**, p.33
drey **12**, p.24
driftwood **110**, p.17
driver's cab **129**, p.35
driver's seat **131**, p.35
drive shaft **135**, p.27
driving wheel **144**, p.35
drogue parachute **123**, p.41

drone pipe, **94**, p.23
droop nose **39**, p.15
drumhead **8**, p.22
drumkit **56**, p.22
drum majorette **133**, p.23
drummer **58**, p.22
drumsticks **2**, p.22
duck **83**, p.13
duckling **84**, p.13
dulcimer **87**, p.23
dumb-bell **65**, p.8
dummy **84**, p.29
dumplings **72**, p.18
dump truck **27**, p.4
dune buggy **74**, p.27
dungeon **92**, p.20
dust guard **67**, p.41
dustpan **132**, p.6
dust rag **130**, p.6
duty free shop **101**, p.14
dye bath **2**, p.32
dynamo **25**, p.26

Ee

earmuffs **90**, p.15
earpiece **79**, p.36
Earth **136**, p.41
earth resources satellite **32**, p.40
easel **48**, p.32
eaves **31**, p.4
éclairs **93**, p.18
eel **67**, p.16
egg case **55**, p.16
eggplant **9**, p.18
eggs **71**, p.12
eggs (fried) **75**, p.18
egg timer **149**, p.7
elbow pad **139**, p.9
electric drill **57**, p.4
electric guitar 71, p.22
electrician **86**, p.5
electricity cable **146**, p.29
electricity meter **114**, p.5
electric locomotive 58, p.34
electric motor **64**, p.35
electric organ **70**, p.22
electric piano **67**, p.22
electric rail **52**, p.34
electric truck **36**, p.34
electric wire **87**, p.5
electronic games **143**, p.31
elephant **151**, p.31
elevator **60**, p.14
elevon **113**, p.41
elf **90**, p.31

embroidery **99**, p.31
emergency button **41**, p.34
emergency exit **71**, p.15
emergency stairs **44**, p.34
engine cowling **98**, p.14
engineer **59**, p.34
engine intake **83**, p.15
engine nozzle **15**, p.40
engine room **102**, p.39
entry/exit platform **53**, p.40
entry hatch **50**, p.40
épée **75**, p.8
escalator **43**, p.34
estate car **87**, p.27
excavator **105**, p.31
executive jet **41**, p.15
exercise bicycle **41**, p.41
exhaust deflector **51**, p.40
exhaust outlet **23**, p.14
exhaust pipe **142**, p.27
exhaust stack **7**, p.38
exit sign **50**, p.34
external tank **122**, p.41
extra-vehicular glove **86**, p.41
ewe **32**, p.12

Ff

faceguard **140**, p.11
face powder **69**, p.36
facia board **30**, p.4
fairway **108**, p.9
fairy **8**, p.30
falcon **144**, p.21
falconer **143**, p.21
falcons' mews **145**, p.21
false beard **63**, p.36
false nose **64**, p.36
false teeth **66**, p.36
fan **48**, p.34
fan air nozzle **31**, p.15
fan belt **107**, p.27
farmer **108**, p.13
farmer's wife **70**, p.12
farmhouse **53**, p.12
farm machinery 137, p.13
farm manager **119**, p.13
farm worker **118**, p.13
father **16**, p.6
fawn **8**, p.24
feathers **90**, p.13
feeder **48**, p.12
felt tip pens **29**, p.30
fence **72**, p.12
fencing 66, p.8
fencing glove **73**, p.8
fencing mask **67**, p.8

fencing master **68**, p.8
fender **80**, p.39
fennel **26**, p.18
ferris wheel **64**, p.30
fertilizer **131**, p.13
field **38**, p.12
fielder **25**, p.10
figs **47**, p.18
file **80**, p.4
filing cabinet **8**, p.36
film camera **135**, p.37
film cassette **120**, p.33
film set **146**, p.37
fin **64**, p.16
fingerboard **84**, p.23
finishing line **14**, p.8
fire **106**, p.29
fireboat **41**, p.38
fire box **124**, p.35
fire engine **89**, p.27
fire escape **8**, p.28
fire extinguisher **39**, p.34
firehood **31**, p.32
firehose **107**, p.29
fire hydrant **122**, p.29
fire irons **30**, p.32
fireman **104**, p.29
fireplace **89**, p.21
firepot **24**, p.21
firescreen **111**, p.21
fire station **4**, p.28
fire tender **138**, p.15
fire tower **105**, p.39
fire tubes **123**, p.35
firewood **117**, p.25
fireworks **49**, p.30
first stage **9**, p.40
fish 116, p.19
fish boxes **92**, p.17
fish cakes **120**, p.19
fisherman **112**, p.17
fish filet **125**, p.19
fish fingers **121**, p.19
fishing boat **113**, p.17
fishing net **70**, p.24
fishing rod **69**, p.24
fishmonger **49**, p.28
fishplate **75**, p.35
fishpond **123**, p.21
fish shop **48**, p.28
fish steak **124**, p.19
fish tank **58**, p.7
flag **68**, p.29
flagpole **69**, p.29
flagstick **111**, p.9
flail **13**, p.21
flare **71**, p.39
flash gun **130**, p.33
flashing **25**, p.4
flashlight **136**, p.31
flash shoe **113**, p.33
flask **43**, p.30

flat car **15**, p.35
flatter **25**, p.32
flautist **40**, p.22
flexible skirt **33**, p.38
flight **39**, p.8
flight deck **87**, p.15
flight engineer **84**, p.15
flight indicator board **109**, p.14
flight information desk **113**, p.14
flight plan **55**, p.14
flipper **100**, p.17
float **45**, p.15
float (tool) **39**, p.4
floodlights **51**, p.14
floorboards **52**, p.4
floor joist **49**, p.4
floor manager **112**, p.37
floor plan **14**, p.36
floor tiles **96**, p.5
floor tom **57**, p.22
florist's **4**, p.38
flour **152**, p.19
flower **84**, p.25
flower bed **54**, p.24
flowerpots **63**, p.32
flower seller **138**, p.29
flute **15**, p.22
flyover **7**, p.28
fly sheet **131**, p.25
foal **81**, p.13
focus control **116**, p.33
focusing handle **119**, p.37
fog horn **89**, p.39
fog signal **84**, p.17
foil **72**, p.8
foldaway bunk **90**, p.35
folding rule **140**, p.5
folk singer **127**, p.23
food processor **147**, p.33
food trolley **69**, p.15
foot brake **127**, p.27
foot pad **57**, p.40
foot pedal **9**, p.22
footprint **73**, p.41
foot pump **140**, p.27
foot rest **65**, p.26
foot soldier **1**, p.20
forage harvester **138**, p.13
forecastle **95**, p.39
foredeck **93**, p.39
foreman **6**, p.4
foresail **67**, p.38
forest **108**, p.25
forester **109**, p.25
fork **143**, p.6
forklift truck **104**, p.35
fort **57**, p.30
foundations **75**, p.4
fountain **94**, p.29
fountain pen **22**, p.30

fox **14**, p.24
fox cubs **13**, p.24
frame **41**, p.26
freezer **80**, p.6
freight car **3**, p.34
freight plane 46, p.15
freight train **2**, p.34
French horn **27**, p.22
French loaf **136**, p.19
freshwater tanker **126**, p.14
frets **74**, p.22
frisbee **94**, p.17
frog **78**, p.25
frogman **123**, p.17
front bumper **104**, p.27
front coupling **71**, p.35
front disc brake **62**, p.26
front fork **42**, p.26
front runner **85**, p.11
front suspension **113**, p.27
front wheel **33**, p.26
front wing **102**, p.27
fruit 36, p.18
fruit bowl **82**, p.6
fruit juice **147**, p.19
fruit picker **102**, p.13
fruit salad **94**, p.18
fruit stall **119**, p.29
fruit tart **99**, p.18
fruit tree **106**, p.21
frying pan **151**, p.7
fuller **24**, p.32
funnel **42**, p.30
funnel (ship's) **88**, p.39
furrows **94**, p.13
fuse box **111**, p.5
fuselage **95**, p.15

Gg

gable end **26**, p.4
gallery **84**, p.20
gantry **3**, p.40
gantry crane **7**, p.34
garage 93, p.27
garbage can **88**, p.6
garden **52**, p.24
gardener 59, p.32
gardening gloves **67**, p.32
garden basket **72**, p.32
garden shed **47**, p.24
garden tools **68**, p.32
garderobe (lavatory) **96**, p.21
garlic **104**, p.19
gas bags **36**, p.15
gas boiler **112**, p.5

gas burner **21**, p.24
gas cap **146**, p.27
gas gauge **120**, p.27
gas lamp **137**, p.25
gas meter **113**, p.5
gas pipe **67**, p.28
gas pump **94**, p.27
gas tank **57**, p.26
gate **41**, p.12
gatehouse **152**, p.21
gate key **153**, p.29
gatepost **96**, p.29
G-cramp **100**, p.33
gear box **129**, p.27
gear cable **12**, p.26
gear change lever **10**, p.26
gear stick **130**, p.27
generator **81**, p.34
genoa **69**, p.38
gherkins **163**, p.19
ghost **82**, p.31
giant clam **118**, p.17
giraffe **154**, p.31
glass **91**, p.6
glass cutter **130**, p.5
glaze **22**, p.32
glazier **126**, p.5
glider **42**, p.15
globe **37**, p.30
glockenspiel **86**, p.23
glove puppet **69**, p.30
gloves **67**, p.26
gnome **91**, p.31
goal **142**, p.11
goal crease **56**, p.10
goal keeper **141**, p.11
goal line **55**, p.10
goal pad **54**, p.10
goal post **18**, p.10
goggles **101**, p.17
go-kart **7**, p.26
golf 100, p.9
golf bag **102**, p.9
golf ball **109**, p.9
golf clubs **101**, p.9
golfer **104**, p.9
golf trolley **105**, p.9
gondola **125**, p.39
gong **98**, p.23
gong (timekeeping) **59**, p.8
goose **87**, p.13
goose barnacle **50**, p.16
gooseberries **63**, p.18
gosling **88**, p.13
gourd **104**, p.23
grab **6**, p.34
gramophone **29**, p.36
grandfather **109**, p.7
grandfather clock **50**, p.6
grandmother **74**, p.6
grapefruit **44**, p.18
grapes **40**, p.18

grass **71**, p.24
grasshopper **77**, p.25
grate **146**, p.35
grater **150**, p.33
grating **154**, p.29
grease paint **65**, p.36
great hall **88**, p.21
great helm **49**, p.20
great oven **108**, p.21
greengages **58**, p.18
greenhouse **48**, p.24
green pepper **34**, p.18
grip **133**, p.9
ground control officer **54**, p.14
guard **110**, p.21
guard rail **110**, p.39
guiro **157**, p.23
guitar pan **147**, p.23
gulley **117**, p.5
gun **144**, p.37
gun carriage **33**, p.21
gunpowder cartridge **31**, p.21
gutter **90**, p.5
guy rope **129**, p.25
gymnasium **79**, p.9
gymnast **77**, p.9

Hh

hacksaw **51**, p.4
hair brush **126**, p.6
hair curlers **57**, p.36
hairdresser **59**, p.28
hair salon **58**, p.28
hairdryer **57**, p.28
half-jacket **70**, p.8
hall 98, p.7
halyard **148**, p.39
ham **110**, p.19
hamburger **76**, p.18
hammer **142**, p.5
hammer thrower **30**, p.8
hammock **110**, p.25
hamster **51**, p.7
handbag **33**, p.34
handbell **110**, p.23
hand brake **131**, p.27
handcuffs **143**, p.37
hand drill **101**, p.33
hand grip **9**, p.26
handlebar **11**, p.26
hand luggage **108**, p.14
hand saw **138**, p.5
handsets **146**, p.31
handstand **98**, p.9
handwheel **70**, p.35

hangar deck **115**, p.39
hang glider **19**, p.24
hardboard **96**, p.33
hardcore **14**, p.4
hare **49**, p.12
harmonica **116**, p.23
harp **45**, p.22
harpist **44**, p.22
harrow **143**, p.13
harvest mouse **16**, p.24
hatch door **28**, p.40
hats **134**, p.29
hawk (bird) **92**, p.25
hawk (tool) **68**, p.4
hawsehole **29**, p.38
hay bale **120**, p.13
hay baler **140**, p.13
hay elevator **147**, p.13
hay loft **114**, p.13
hay net **51**, p.12
hay rake **7**, p.12
haystack **95**, p.13
headboard **19**, p.6
head-dress **53**, p.30
header tank **102**, p.5
headguard **52**, p.8
headlamp **105**, p.27
headphones **71**, p.36
headrest **125**, p.27
headstand **93**, p.9
headstock **72**, p.22
heat insulation tiles **95**, p.41
heatshield **24**, p.40
hedge **45**, p.12
hedge cutter **107**, p.13
hedgehog **2**, p.24
hedgerow **105**, p.25
helicopter 19, p.14
helmsman **131**, p.39
herald **67**, p.20
herb bed **104**, p.21
herbs 101, p.19
hermit crab **57**, p.16
hen **92**, p.13
hen house **47**, p.12
high board **143**, p.9
high chair **11**, p.7
high-gain antenna **61**, p.41
high jump **20**, p.8
high kick **46**, p.8
hihat **61**, p.22
hiker **64**, p.24
hill **93**, p.25
hinge **116**, p.35
hinged bow **123**, p.39
hinged nose **47**, p.15
hippopotamus **152**, p.31
historical costume **39**, p.36
hoarding **151**, p.21
hobby horse **109**, p.31
hockey 139, p.11

hockey stick **143**, p.11
hod **63**, p.4
hoe **2**, p.12
holster **139**, p.37
home plate **46**, p.10
honey **156**, p.19
hood **40**, p.20
hoof **130**, p.13
hoop **125**, p.11
horizontal bar **89**, p.9
horn (of animal) **78**, p.13
horn (bicycle) **20**, p.26
horse **124**, p.13
horse armor **62**, p.21
horse jump **72**, p.10
horse racing 58, p.10
horse rider **127**, p.13
horseshoeing box **36**, p.32
hose **64**, p.12
hosereels **42**, p.38
hospital **74**, p.29
hot-air balloon **20**, p.24
hot chocolate **140**, p.19
hot dogs **79**, p.18
hotel **9**, p.28
hotel reservations **115**, p.15
hot water pipe , **105**, p.5
hot water tank **106**, p.5
hounds **134**, p.21
house **50**, p.24
hovercraft 30, p.38
hulahoop **112**, p.31
hull **99**, p.39
hurdle **18**, p.8
hurdler **17**, p.8
hut **137**, p.21
hydraulic fork **63**, p.26
hydraulic lift **99**, p.27
hydrofoil **35**, p.38

Ii

ice box **134**, p.25
ice cream **86**, p.18
ice cream stall **7**, p.16
ice hockey 51, p.10
ice removal vehicle **135**, p.15
ice skate **52**, p.10
icing **133**, p.19
immigration officer **121**, p.15
Indian brave **59**, p.30
Indian chief **54**, p.30
indicator light **145**, p.27
infantry men **103**, p.31

inflatable liferaft **111**, p.39
inflight antenna **48**, p.40
information office **27**, p.34
inner bailey **116**, p.21
inner tube **47**, p.26
inspection bay **96**, p.27
inspection pit **120**, p.5
instructor **91**, p.9
instrument panel 1, p.14
instrument unit **13**, p.40
insulator **60**, p.34
iron (electric) **83**, p.6
iron (metal) **32**, p.32
ironing board **84**, p.6
island **89**, p.17
i.v. drip **95**, p.37

Jj

jack (car) **152**, p.27
jack (in bowls) **96**, p.11
jack (ship's flag) **97**, p.39
jack-in-the-box **61**, p.30
jack plug socket **79**, p.22
jackstaff **98**, p.39
jai-alai 132, p.11
jai-alai court **134**, p.11
jailer **95**, p.20
jam **151**, p.19
javelin **26**, p.8
jazz band 117, p.23
jazz singer **120**, p.23
jelly **90**, p.18
jellyfish **62**, p.16
jersey **131**, p.29
jester **99**, p.21
jet engine **97**, p.15
jet plane 59, p.14
jets (fighter) **118**, p.39
jetty **109**, p.17
jeweler's saw **159**, p.33
jib **138**, p.39
jib sheet **146**, p.39
jigsaw puzzle **124**, p.31
jingles **152**, p.23
jockey **62**, p.10
jodhpurs **74**, p.10
jousting tournament 56, p.20
judge **57**, p.8
judo 48, p.8
judoka **50**, p.8
jumping ramp **117**, p.9
jumping sheet **108**, p.29
jump jet 27, p.15
junk **129**, p.39
Jupiter **138**, p.41

Kk

kale **17**, p.12
kaleidoscope **46**, p.30
kangaroo **77**, p.30
karabiner **30**, p.24
karate 45, p.8
karate suit **47**, p.8
kayak **66**, p.10
keel **70**, p.38
keep **72**, p.20
keeper-of-the-hounds **135**, p.21
kennel **65**, p.12
kettle **158**, p.7
kettle drum **7**, p.22
kettle hat **3**, p.20
keyboard **115**, p.23
key ring **134**, p.31
keys **135**, p.31
keys (oboe) **13**, p.22
kicking strap **154**, p.39
kickstand **39**, p.26
kick start lever **60**, p.26
kick tail **140**, p.9
kid **77**, p.13
kiln **13**, p.32
king **5**, p.30
kingpost **107**, p.39
kippers **119**, p.19
kitchen 61, p.6
kitchen cabinet **69**, p.6
kitchen shed **102**, p.21
kite **40**, p.24
kitten **55**, p.12
knee pad **141**, p.9
knife **142**, p.6
knight **36**, p.20
knitting needle **101**, p.31
koala bear **153**, p.31
koto **100**, p.23

Ll

lacrosse 39, p.10
ladder **116**, p.13
ladle **153**, p.7
ladybird **75**, p.25
lake **103**, p.25
lamb **31**, p.12
lamp **23**, p.6
lampshade **7**, p.6
lampstand **8**, p.6

lance **54**, p.20
lancet window **73**, p.20
landing **42**, p.34
landing flap **18**, p.14
landing gear **54**, p.40
landing light **93**, p.15
landing mat **95**, p.9
land rover **76**, p.27
lanes **147**, p.9
lantern **50**, p.30
lantern mast **46**, p.38
lasso **145**, p.37
latch **128**, p.5
launch escape tower **17**, p.40
launching catapult **116**, p.39
launching trolley **83**, p.39
launch pad **5**, p.40
launch support **120**, p.41
laundress **124**, p.21
laundry basket **47**, p.6
laundry room **22**, p.38
lavatory **46**, p.6
lavatory cleaning vehicle **133**, p.15
lawn **55**, p.24
lawn mower **71**, p.32
lead guitarist **69**, p.22
leading wheel **136**, p.35
leeks **12**, p.18
left luggage office **25**, p.34
leggings **39**, p.20
lemons **42**, p.18
lemon squeezer **144**, p.33
lens **117**, p.33
leopard **79**, p.30
leotard **80**, p.9
letterbox **25**, p.28
letters **31**, p.30
lettuce **27**, p.18
library **18**, p.38
lido **2**, p.38
lifebelt **11**, p.16
lifeboats **87**, p.39
lifeboat station **85**, p.17
life buoy **73**, p.39
lifeguard **5**, p.16
lift **40**, p.34
light aircraft 13, p.14
light fittings **98**, p.5
lighthouse **87**, p.17
lighting director **134**, p.37
lighting tower **9**, p.34
lightning rod **1**, p.40
light screen **118**, p.33
lightship **45**, p.38
lily pad **80**, p.25
limes **41**, p.18
limpets **49**, p.16
line and pins **70**, p.4
linen closet **34**, p.6

linesman **122**, p.9
linoleum **124**, p.5
lintel **50**, p.4
lion **150**, p.31
lip plate **30**, p.22
lipstick **68**, p.36
liquid oxygen tank **11**, p.40
litter **81**, p.29
litter basket **142**, p.29
living room 103, p.7
loading foreman **16**, p.35
lobby **15**, p.28
lobster **60**, p.16
lobster pot **108**, p.17
lock **102**, p.25
loft window **15**, p.4
log cabin **101**, p.25
logs **133**, p.21
longbow **11**, p.20
long jump **19**, p.8
lookout tower **10**, p.38
loom **3**, p.32
loudspeaker **24**, p.34
low-gain antenna **62**, p.41
luggage **106**, p.35
luggage carousel **119**, p.15
luggage rack **100**, p.35
luggage reclaim hall **120**, p.15
lugworm **104**, p.17
lug wrench **151**, p.27
lunar module 45, p.40
lunar module hangar **14**, p.40
lunar overshoe **90**, p.41
lunar rover **60**, p.41
lunar surface **59**, p.40
lunch box **132**, p.31
lute **108**, p.23
lychees **51**, p.18

Mm

mace **14**, p.21
magazine rack **111**, p.7
magazines **29**, p.34
magnet **36**, p.30
magnetometer **114**, p.41
magnifying glass **44**, p.30
maid **77**, p.20
mailbags **55**, p.34
mail van **28**, p.28
main recovery parachute **21**, p.40
mainsail **136**, p.39
main sheet **152**, p.39
maintenance engineer **99**, p.14

main wheels **111**, p.41
maize **19**, p.12
make-up artist **56**, p.36
make-up box **67**, p.36
mallet **152**, p.5
man **147**, p.29
manager **60**, p.8
mandolin **89**, p.23
mandrel **37**, p.32
mane **125**, p.13
maneuvering engine **119**, p.41
mangoes **45**, p.18
mangonel **23**, p.21
manhole **145**, p.29
manhole cover **141**, p.29
mantlet **21**, p.21
manure **145**, p.13
manure spreader **146**, p.13
map **127**, p.25
maracas **154**, p.23
marathon runner **10**, p.8
marbles **117**, p.31
mare **80**, p.13
marimba **106**, p.23
marksman **103**, p.11
marmalade **168**, p.19
Mars **135**, p.41
marshaller **89**, p.15
marshalling yard 1, p.34
masking tape **156**, p.5
masks **24**, p.36
mast **135**, p.39
material **88**, p.33
mattress **97**, p.9
mayonnaise **157**, p.19
measuring cup **146**, p.33
meat 109, p.19
meat pie **70**, p.18
mechanic **98**, p.27
mechanical arm **79**, p.16
medals **47**, p.36
medicine bottle **89**, p.37
medicine cabinet **37**, p.6
megaphone **3**, p.16
melody pipe **91**, p.23
melons **52**, p.18
menu **92**, p.35
merchant **114**, p.21
Mercury **133**, p.41
meringues **98**, p.18
merlon **149**, p.21
metal ruler **99**, p.33
meteorite **125**, p.41
metronome **125**, p.23
micrometeoroid shield **38**, p.40
microphone **63**, p.22
microphone **107**, p.37
microphone boom **106**, p.37
microscope **45**, p.30

milk **122**, p.13
milking machine **134**, p.13
milk jug **93**, p.6
milkshake **148**, p.19
milk tanker **121**, p.13
Milky Way **127**, p.41
mini submarine **126**, p.17
minstrel **85**, p.20
mint **105**, p.19
mirror **15**, p.6
mirror lights **53**, p.36
mitre block **106**, p.33
mitre cramp **102**, p.33
mitt **45**, p.10
mixing bowl **149**, p.33
mobile **18**, p.30
mobile generator **128**, p.14
model **42**, p.32
modeling clay **62**, p.36
modeling tools **15**, p.32
mole **62**, p.24
mole hill **61**, p.24
money **98**, p.31
money bag **152**, p.37
money box **63**, p.30
monitor screen **128**, p.37
monk **131**, p.21
monkey **80**, p.30
monster **88**, p.31
moog synthesiser **68**, p.22
Moon **141**, p.41
moon crater **75**, p.41
moon dust **74**, p.41
moon rock **58**, p.40
moonwalk **92**, p.41
mooring winch **106**, p.39
mop **86**, p.37
moped **6**, p.26
mortar **44**, p.4
moss **142**, p.25
moth **140**, p.25
mother **52**, p.7
motorbike 52, p.26
motor boat **119**, p.9
motor boat **36**, p.38
motor cyclist **98**, p.29
motor scooter **5**, p.26
moulding **107**, p.33
mountain **3**, p.10
mounting board **98**, p.33
mousse **91**, p.18
moustaches **58**, p.36
mouthpiece **26**, p.22
moving van, **80**, p.26
moving walkway **123**, p.15
mowing machine **46**, p.12
mud **67**, p.12
mudguard **31**, p.26
muffins **130**, p.19
muffler **66**, p.26
muffler **133**, p.27
mural **21**, p.28

mushrooms **21**, p.18
music box **62**, p.30
music stand **48**, p.22
mussels **46**, p.16
mustard **153**, p.19
mustard plant **16**, p.12
muzzle **32**, p.21

Nn

nails **153**, p.5
nanny **92**, p.29
nanny goat **76**, p.13
napkin **92**, p.6
national flag **64**, p.14
navigation bridge and
　chartroom **11**, p.38
navigator **128**, p.17
neck **73**, p.22
necklace **164**, p.33
needles **87**, p.33
neon sign **43**, p.28
Neptune **143**, p.41
nest **97**, p.25
nestlings **96**, p.25
net **93**, p.17
newel post **36**, p.4
newsagent **28**, p.34
newscaster **80**, p.36
newspaper **53**, p.28
newspaper stand **54**, p.28
nightclub **9**, p.38
nobles **60**, p.21
nose cap **94**, p.41
nose cone **35**, p.15
nose ring **30**, p.12
nose wheels **92**, p.15
notebook **32**, p.30
number plate **141**, p.27
numbers **30**, p.30
nun **130**, p.21
nurse **90**, p.37
nuts **160**, p.19

Oo

oar **150**, p.11
oarsman **151**, p.11
oats **15**, p.12
oboe **12**, p.22
observation terrace **56**,
　p.14
ocean liner 1, p.38
octopus **71**, p.16

office **20**, p.28
office building **17**, p.28
oil can **149**, p.27
oil cooler **62**, p.34
oil filter **117**, p.27
oil paints **45**, p.32
oil pan **118**, p.27
omelette **74**, p.18
onions **20**, p.18
open goods wagon **10**,
　p.34
optical sight **101**, p.11
oranges **43**, p.18
orbital workshop **39**, p.41
orchard **103**, p.13
orchestra 32, p.22
organ **35**, p.22
organ pipes **37**, p.22
ostrich **155**, p.31
otter **1**, p.24
outboard motor **38**, p.38
outer bailey **128**, p.21
outfielder **47**, p.10
outrigger **65**, p.38
outrigger wheel **28**, p.15
oven **75**, p.6
overall **132**, p.13
overflow pipe **108**, p.5
overhead light **82**, p.37
overhead wire **66**, p.35
oxidizer tank **97**, p.41
oxygen tube **140**, p.17
oysters **39**, p.16

Pp

packhorse **113**, p.21
padded couch **26**, p.40
paddle **79**, p.39
paddling pool **57**, p.24
paddock **40**, p.12
page **16**, p.30
paint (house) **145**, p.5
paintbox **44**, p.32
paintbrush **146**, p.5
painter **144**, p.5
painting knife **56**, p.32
paintings **126**, p.29
paint roller **147**, p.5
paint tray **148**, p.5
paint trolley **10**, p.36
palette **52**, p.32
palette knife **54**, p.32
pallet **110**, p.41
pallet (mattress) **83**, p.20
pancakes **77**, p.18
panda **73**, p.30

panniers **34**, p.26
pantograph **65**, p.35
paper hats **48**, p.30
papoose **56**, p.30
parallel bars **88**, p.9
parcels **27**, p.28
park **95**, p.29
park bench **91**, p.29
parking meter **90**, p.29
parrot **19**, p.30
parsley **106**, p.19
parsnip **8**, p.18
passenger bridge **57**, p.14
passenger bus **136**, p.15
passenger cabin **82**, p.15
passenger car **98**, p.35
passengers **102**, p.29
passenger seat **56**, p.26
passenger steps **34**, p.38
passenger terminal 100,
　p.14
passenger train 88, p.35
passport **105**, p.14
passport control **122**, p.15
pastry **97**, p.18
pastry brush **140**, p.33
patchwork quilt **53**, p.7
pâté **87**, p.18
path **67**, p.24
pavement **123**, p.29
pavilion **59**, p.20
paving stones **135**, p.5
paw paws **46**, p.18
payload bay **103**, p.41
payload bay door **104**, p.41
payload specialists **106**,
　p.41
peaches **54**, p.18
peacock **75**, p.12
peanut butter **161**, p.19
pears **48**, p.18
peas **3**, p.18
peasant **122**, p.21
pedal **37**, p.26
pedal boat **8**, p.16
pedal crank **38**, p.26
pedestal **120**, p.37
pedestrian **144**, p.29
pegbox **109**, p.23
pelote (ball) **135**, p.11
pencil case **21**, p.30
pencils **24**, p.30
pendulum **126**, p.23
penguins **76**, p.30
penknife **133**, p.31
penlight pocket **84**, p.41
pennant **81**, p.39
pepper **155**, p.19
peppermill **155**, p.7
perch **142**, p.21
percussion **38**, p.22
periwinkle **54**, p.16

pheasant **76**, p.25
phone booth **63**, p.28
photograph booth **109**,
　p.35
photographer 108, p.33
photograph frame **105**, p.7
pianist **123**, p.23
piano **124**, p.23
piccolo **29**, p.22
pickaxe **74**, p.4
pickup **76**, p.22
picnic hamper **24**, p.16
picnic table **119**, p.25
picture framer 95, p.33
picture glass **97**, p.33
pigeon **74**, p.25
piglet **37**, p.12
pigsty **57**, p.12
pike **4**, p.20
pillar **55**, p.28
pillow **24**, p.6
pills **104**, p.37
pilot **86**, p.15
pilot house **49**, p.38
pilot's seat **98**, p.41
pincer **61**, p.16
pin cushion **93**, p.33
pineapple **37**, p.18
pine cone **10**, p.24
ping pongs **146**, p.23
pins **92**, p.33
pipefish **114**, p.17
piping bag **138**, p.33
pirate **86**, p.31
piste **7**, p.10
pistol **85**, p.31
piston **115**, p.27
piston rod **139**, p.35
pita bread **138**, p.19
pitch **109**, p.11
pitcher **50**, p.10
pitcher's mound **49**, p.10
pitchfork **4**, p.12
pitch thrusters **27**, p.40
piton **29**, p.24
piton hammer **34**, p.24
pitot head **32**, p.15
pizza **83**, p.18
place mat **90**, p.6
plane **137**, p.5
planet **128**, p.41
plank **55**, p.4
plans **9**, p.4
plant **53**, p.24
plant cover **62**, p.32
plaster **42**, p.4
plasterboard **40**, p.4
plaster cast **96**, p.37
plasterer **38**, p.4
plate **128**, p.6
plate armor **43**, p.20
platform **54**, p.34

platform number **34**, p.34
playing cards **119**, p.31
playpen **9**, p.6
pliers **161**, p.33
plough **144**, p.13
plumber **76**, p.4
plumb line **69**, p.4
plume **58**, p.20
plums **55**, p.18
Pluto **144**, p.41
plywood **37**, p.4
pogo stick **110**, p.31
pointing knife **73**, p.4
polar bear **72**, p.30
pole vault **24**, p.8
police launch **44**, p.38
policeman **61**, p.28
polish **131**, p.6
polishing machine **158**, p.33
polo 128, p.11
polo pony **130**, p.11
polo stick **129**, p.11
pommel horse **90**, p.9
pommel saddle **64**, p.20
pond **74**, p.12
pony riders **106**, p.25
poop deck **85**, p.39
porch **60**, p.6
porpoise **119**, p.17
portable life support system **80**, p.41
portcullis **153**, p.21
portholes **27**, p.38
portrait **97**, p.6
port side **133**, p.39
Portuguese-man-of-war **43**, p.16
post **107**, p.17
post-and-rails **70**, p.10
poster **117**, p.29
poster paints **28**, p.30
postman **26**, p.28
post office **23**, p.28
potato chips **78**, p.18
potatoes **5**, p.18
potato harvester **148**, p.13
potato rake **6**, p.12
potter 12, p.32
potter's knife **17**, p.32
potter's wheel **20**, p.32
powder puff **70**, p.36
powerboat **40**, p.38
power line **99**, p.25
power station **104**, p.25
power unit **127**, p.33
prawns **118**, p.19
present **97**, p.37
presser foot **83**, p.33
pressure hull **145**, p.17
pressurized helmet **81**, p.41
prince **4**, p.30

princess **3**, p.30
prints **132**, p.33
prisoner **93**, p.20
producer **3**, p.36
production assistant **130**, p.37
production control room 125, p.37
profile board **11**, p.4
promenade **12**, p.16
propane torch **155**, p.33
propeller blade **14**, p.14
propeller shaft **100**, p.39
prop master **22**, p.36
prop store 20, p.36
pruning shears **78**, p.32
puck **57**, p.10
pulley **45**, p.4
pumpkin **19**, p.18
punchbag **63**, p.8
punchball **64**, p.8
puncture repair kit **48**, p.26
punt **128**, p.39
puppet theatre **67**, p.30
puppies **66**, p.12
purse **97**, p.31
putting green **110**, p.9
putty **127**, p.5
puzzle **126**, p.31
pylon **100**, p.25

Qq

quarrel **7**, p.20
quarry **98**, p.25
queen **7**, p.30
queue **45**, p.28
quiche **84**, p.18
quilted vest **37**, p.20
quintain **57**, p.20
quiver **9**, p.20

Rr

rabbit **68**, p.12
rabbit hutch **69**, p.12
racehorse **60**, p.10
race track **107**, p.31
race walker **25**, p.8
racing bike **4**, p.26
racing car **71**, p.27
racing colors **59**, p.10

racing yacht **68**, p.38
radar **52**, p.14
radiator **85**, p.5
radiator fan **86**, p.34
radio **138**, p.31
radio aerial **50**, p.14
radio compass **5**, p.14
radio telephone **80**, p.34
radio telescope **2**, p.40
radishes **28**, p.18
radome **91**, p.15
raft **90**, p.17
rafter **21**, p.4
rag **47**, p.32
rag doll **2**, p.30
rail **74**, p.35
railings **97**, p.29
railway map **113**, p.35
railway track **57**, p.34
rain **26**, p.24
rain barrel **61**, p.12
rainbow **24**, p.24
raincoat **44**, p.36
rainwater pipe **110**, p.5
raisins **169**, p.19
ram **33**, p.12
rammer **35**, p.21
ramp **87**, p.29
rape **22**, p.12
raspberries **62**, p.18
rat **115**, p.13
rattle **97**, p.23
rattle (baby's) **131**, p.31
ratchet **6**, p.32
ray **66**, p.16
razor shells **36**, p.16
rear brake pedal **64**, p.26
rear bumper **143**, p.27
rear drum brake **61**, p.26
rear lamp **24**, p.26
rear light **144**, p.27
rear reflector **23**, p.26
rear runner **81**, p.11
rearview mirror **55**, p.26
rearview window **101**, p.41
rear wheel **35**, p.26
reception **14**, p.28
reclining seats **72**, p.15
record deck **106**, p.7
recorder **112**, p.23
record player **139**, p.31
records **141**, p.23
recovery beacon **19**, p.40
red cabbage **18**, p.18
redcurrants **59**, p.18
red pepper **33**, p.18
reed **14**, p.22
reeds **73**, p.12
reed switch **64**, p.22
referee **54**, p.8
refrigerator **79**, p.6
refueller **125**, p.14

registration number **66**, p.14
regulator **127**, p.35
reindeer **95**, p.31
reins **128**, p.13
relay race **31**, p.8
remote control car **106**, p.31
rendezvous radar antenna **47**, p.40
rendezvous window **29**, p.40
rescue launch 109, p.39
restaurant **25**, p.38
retro-rockets **8**, p.40
reversing lever **128**, p.35
reversing light **139**, p.27
revolving door **82**, p.29
rewind lever **114**, p.33
rhinoceros **74**, p.30
rhubarb **32**, p.18
rhythm section **149**, p.23
rice **71**, p.18
rider **99**, p.29
ridge board **22**, p.4
ridge tile **10**, p.4
riding boot **73**, p.10
riding hat **75**, p.10
rifle **102**, p.11
rifle range **105**, p.11
rifle shooting 100, p.11
ring (jewelry) **163**, p.33
rings (in gymnastics) **87**, p.9
rink **90**, p.11
riser **33**, p.4
river **123**, p.25
river bank **113**, p.25
road drill **13**, p.4
road sign **60**, p.28
road sweeper **79**, p.29
robot **130**, p.31
robot arm **108**, p.41
rock **31**, p.16
rock climber **33**, p.24
rocket engines **7**, p.40
rocket thrusters **96**, p.41
rock group 54, p.22
rocking chair **56**, p.7
rocking horse **66**, p.30
rock pool 35, p.16
rock tongs **69**, p.41
roller **136**, p.13
rollerskate **136**, p.9
rollerskater **135**, p.9
rolling pin **136**, p.33
roll thrusters **25**, p.40
roof **2**, p.6
roof cable **61**, p.34
roofing felt **17**, p.4
roof insulation **97**, p.5

roof ladder **19**, p.4
roof rack **97**, p.27
roof terrace **39**, p.28
roots **141**, p.25
rope **99**, p.9
rope wad **25**, p.21
rose **76**, p.32
rosemary **107**, p.19
rostrum **51**, p.22
rotor blade **25**, p.14
rotor hub **24**, p.14
rough **113**, p.9
roundel **47**, p.20
rowing 147, p.11
rowing boat **126**, p.39
rowlock **127**, p.39
rubber **26**, p.30
rubber innersuit **89**, p.41
rubble **131**, p.5
rudder **62**, p.14
rudder blade **149**, p.39
rudder pedal **12**, p.14
rug **117**, p.7
rug beater **10**, p.32
rugby 35, p.10
rugby ball **38**, p.10
ruler **27**, p.30
rungs **88**, p.5
running track **6**, p.8
runway **80**, p.15
runway lights **79**, p.15
rye **12**, p.12

Ss

sabaton **46**, p.20
sabre **76**, p.8
sacks **106**, p.13
saddle **126**, p.13
saddle (bicycle) **16**, p.26
saddle bag **15**, p.26
safelight **124**, p.33
safety cage **29**, p.8
safety net **120**, p.39
safety valves **125**, p.35
sail bag **75**, p.39
sailfish **68**, p.16
sailing dinghy 130, p.39
sailor **17**, p.30
salad **66**, p.18
salami **113**, p.19
salt **154**, p.19
salt-cellar **154**, p.7
sample bag dispenser **68**, p.41
sand **27**, p.16
sand bag **23**, p.24

sandcastle **33**, p.16
sand dunes **83**, p.17
sandpaper **158**, p.5
sand pipe **138**, p.35
sand pit **56**, p.24
sandwiches **82**, p.18
Santa Claus **93**, p.31
sardines **122**, p.19
Saturn **140**, p.41
Saturn's rings **139**, p.41
saucepan **150**, p.7
saucer **124**, p.6
sausages **115**, p.19
sawfish **117**, p.17
saxophone **119**, p.23
scaffolding **61**, p.4
scale armor **42**, p.20
scales **145**, p.33
scallop **59**, p.16
scanner **4**, p.34
scar **59**, p.36
scarecrow **93**, p.13
scarf **84**, p.37
scenery **12**, p.36
scenery builder **17**, p.36
scene shifter **100**, p.37
scenic artist **11**, p.36
school **75**, p.29
school children **77**, p.29
school teacher **76**, p.29
schooner **66**, p.38
scissor-lift transporter **132**, p.15
scissors **86**, p.33
scones **137**, p.19
scoop **72**, p.41
scooter **113**, p.31
scoreboard **43**, p.8
scorer **42**, p.8
scrambler bike **3**, p.26
scratchplate **76**, p.22
screed **58**, p.4
screwdriver **150**, p.5
screws **151**, p.5
script **4**, p.36
scroll **23**, p.22
scroll dog **28**, p.32
scroll iron **27**, p.32
scrubbing brush **133**, p.6
scrum **36**, p.10
scrum half **37**, p.10
scuppers **43**, p.38
scythe **8**, p.12
sea **99**, p.16
sea anemone **42**, p.16
sea bed **147**, p.17
seagull **102**, p.17
seahorse **115**, p.17
seal **17**, p.16
sea lettuce **44**, p.16
seaplane 43, p.15
seal pup **18**, p.16

searchlight **50**, p.38
searchlight (underwater) **78**, p.16
sea scooter **136**, p.17
sea serpent **120**, p.17
sea slug **53**, p.16
sea squirts **37**, p.16
seat **101**, p.35
seat belt **124**, p.27
seat stem **17**, p.26
sea urchin **66**, p.16
seaweed **65**, p.16
seawing **44**, p.15
second **61**, p.8
second stage **10**, p.40
security check **103**, p.14
security guard **37**, p.28
security van **38**, p.28
seed drill **141**, p.13
seedlings **73**, p.32
seed tray **74**, p.32
self-service counter **108**, p.35
semi-truck **91**, p.27
sensor **115**, p.41
sentry **148**, p.21
server **131**, p.9
service box **114**, p.11
service line **128**, p.9
service module **16**, p.40
service station **6**, p.28
set designer **16**, p.36
set model **19**, p.36
sextant **72**, p.39
sewage **150**, p.29
sewer **151**, p.29
sewing box **89**, p.33
sewing machine **80**, p.33
shaft **118**, p.11
shampoo **127**, p.6
shark **121**, p.17
shave hook **78**, p.4
shawl **35**, p.36
shears **70**, p.32
sheath **51**, p.20
shed **50**, p.12
sheep **99**, p.13
sheep dip **101**, p.13
sheep dog **98**, p.13
sheet **20**, p.6
sheet music **50**, p.22
shelf **110**, p.7
shelter **39**, p.12
shepherd **97**, p.13
sheriff **138**, p.37
shield **55**, p.20
shin guard **53**, p.20
shipwreck **132**, p.17
shirt **25**, p.6
shish kebabs **92**, p.18
shoemaker **125**, p.21
shoes **114**, p.29

shoe stall **113**, p.29
shop assistant **50**, p.28
shopping arcade **5**, p.38
shop sign **47**, p.28
shot put **28**, p.8
shoulder pad **16**, p.10
shovel **47**, p.4
shower **35**, p.6
show jumping 69, p.10
shrew **4**, p.24
shrimp **52**, p.16
shrimper **9**, p.16
shrimping net **16**, p.16
shutter **54**, p.12
shutter button **111**, p.33
shutter speed control **112**, p.33
shuttlecock **146**, p.11
sickle **5**, p.12
sidecar **73**, p.27
side light **103**, p.27
siege tower **16**, p.21
sieve **134**, p.33
signal box **11**, p.35
signalman **12**, p.35
signals **20**, p.35
signpost **66**, p.24
sill **56**, p.4
silo **96**, p.13
silver **152**, p.33
silversmith 151, p.33
single berth cabin **15**, p.38
singles sideline **127**, p.9
sink **71**, p.6
siphon **72**, p.16
siren **5**, p.28
sitar **103**, p.23
site hut **7**, p.4
skateboard **142**, p.9
skeg **77**, p.11
skeleton **21**, p.36
sketch pad **49**, p.32
ski **12**, p.10
ski boot **13**, p.10
ski class **8**, p.10
skid landing gear **26**, p.14
skier **6**, p.10
skiff **148**, p.11
skiing 1, p.10
ski instructor **9**, p.10
ski jump **2**, p.10
skip **132**, p.5
skip (captain) **88**, p.11
ski pole **14**, p.10
skipping rope **114**, p.31
skirting board **123**, p.5
sky **91**, p.25
skycrane **37**, p.15
skylight **22**, p.28
skyscraper **1**, p.28
slalom course **11**, p.10

sledge hammer **38**, p.32
sleep compartment **40**, p.41
sleeper **72**, p.35
sleeping bag **136**, p.25
sleeping
    compartment **89**, p.35
sleeve **45**, p.36
sleigh **92**, p.31
sleigh bells **111**, p.23
slide **58**, p.24
slide (trombone) **5**, p.22
slide projector **129**, p.33
sling **19**, p.21
slippers **29**, p.6
slipway **86**, p.17
sloop **60**, p.38
slug **3**, p.24
smithy **120**, p.21
smock **46**, p.32
smoke **103**, p.29
smokebox **119**, p.35
smokebox door **115**, p.35
smoke deflector **8**, p.38
smoked salmon **117**, p.19
smoke hole **119**, p.21
smokestack **117**, p.35
snail **90**, p.25
snake **158**, p.31
snare drum **3**, p.22
snooker ball **128**, p.31
snooker table **127**, p.31
snorkel **91**, p.17
snout **35**, p.12
snow blower **130**, p.14
soap **120**, p.6
soccer 19, p.10
soccer ball **22**, p.10
socket **122**, p.5
socks **136**, p.29
sofa **108**, p.7
solar **71**, p.20
solar flare **132**, p.41
solar panel **37**, p.40
solar shield **36**, p.40
solar system **129**, p.41
solar wing **42**, p.41
soldering iron **77**, p.4
solid rocket booster **121**, p.41
somersault **96**, p.9
son **41**, p.6
sorting office **24**, p.28
soufflé **89**, p.18
soundboard **130**, p.23
sound control room 122, p.37
sound engineer **124**, p.37
soundhole **129**, p.23
sound recordist **147**, p.37
sound supervisor **123**, p.37
sound technician **110**, p.37
soup **73**, p.18
soup bowl **129**, p.6
souvenir stall **115**, p.29

sow **36**, p.12
space laboratory **107**, p.41
space launch station **4**,
    p.40
space probe **33**, p.40
space radiator **105**, p.41
space rocket 6, p.40
spaceship **108**, p.31
space shuttle 93, p.41
space station 35, p.40
spacesuit **82**, p.41
space telescope **109**, p.41
spacewalk **117**, p.41
spade **9**, p.12; **34**, p.16
spaghetti **68**, p.18
Spanish guitar **128**, p.23
spanners **50**, p.26
spare wheel **138**, p.27
spark plug **58**, p.26
spatula **139**, p.33
speaker **55**, p.22
speargun **133**, p.17
spectacles **51**, p.36
spectators **8**, p.8
speedball **62**, p.8
speed brake **118**, p.41
speedometer **119**, p.27
spider **88**, p.25
spider crab **51**, p.16
spike **76**, p.35
spinach **2**, p.18
spines **69**, p.16
spinnaker **61**, p.38
spinnaker boom **62**, p.38
spinner **15**, p.14
spinning top **115**, p.31
spiral staircase **90**, p.21
spire **41**, p.24
spirit burner **40**, p.30
spirit level **72**, p.4
spit **109**, p.21
splashpan **21**, p.32
spoiler **76**, p.15
spoke reflector **46**, p.26
spokes **45**, p.26
sponge **81**, p.16
spoon **144**, p.6
sports car **70**, p.27
sports deck **3**, p.38
spotlight **43**, p.37
springboard **84**, p.9
sprinter **2**, p.8
sprocket **26**, p.26
spurs **140**, p.37
squash 110, p.11
squash ball **112**, p.11
squash court **111**, p.11
squash racket **113**, p.11
squaw **55**, p.30
squid **80**, p.16
squire **38**, p.20
squirrel **11**, p.24

stabilizer **21**, p.14
stable **52**, p.12
stable boy **141**, p.21
stadium **5**, p.8
stag **5**, p.24
stagecoach **150**, p.37
staircase **32**, p.4
stairs (wooden) **115**, p.21
stairwell **117**, p.21
stall **112**, p.13
stamp **26**, p.32
stapler **51**, p.32
star **126**, p.41
starboard side **151**, p.39
starfish **58**, p.16
starter **149**, p.9
starting block **1**, p.8
starting gun **11**, p.8
staterooms **16**, p.38
station 22, p.34
station clock **23**, p.34
statue **32**, p.28
stay **134**, p.39
steak **114**, p.19
steam dome **121**, p.35
steam engine 114, p.35
steamroller **4**, p.4
steel band 142, p.23
steel drum **143**, p.23
steel girder **47**, p.34
steeplechaser **16**, p.8
steering arm **39**, p.38
steering wheel **122**, p.27
step ladder **91**, p.5
steps **65**, p.28
stereo **107**, p.7
stern **140**, p.39
stethoscope **54**, p.36
stetson **137**, p.37
stew **67**, p.18
steward **129**, p.21
stewardess **94**, p.15
stick glove **53**, p.10
sticking plaster **103**, p.37
stilts **111**, p.31
stirrup **129**, p.13
stirrup (on crossbow) **6**,
    p.20
stones **156**, p.33
stool **87**, p.6
stopcock **118**, p.5
stops **36**, p.22
stop watch **129**, p.37
store room **42**, p.28
straight edge **41**, p.4
straw **113**, p.13
strawberries **61**, p.18
street lamp **73**, p.29
street map **139**, p.29
street musician **45**, p.34
street sign **56**, p.28
stretcher **120**, p.29

striker **21**, p.10
string puppet **68**, p.30
strings **82**, p.23
string section **43**, p.22
striplight **14**, p.6
stripping knife **159**, p.5
strobe light **126**, p.33
stroller **88**, p.29
strut **20**, p.4
studio 81, p.37
studio camera **109**, p.37
studio monitor **114**, p.37
stuffing **81**, p.18
stumps **32**, p.10
stuntman **151**, p.37
suckers **73**, p.16
sugar **150**, p.19
sugar beet **21**, p.12
sugar bowl **137**, p.6
suitcase **13**, p.28
Sun **131**, p.41
sun deck **6**, p.38
sunflower **18**, p.12
sunglasses pocket **77**, p.41
sun hat **14**, p.16
sunspot **130**, p.41
supermarket **41**, p.28
supersonic airliner 38, p.15
supervisor's van **75**, p.15
surf **103**, p.17
surfboard **78**, p.11
surfing 76, p.11
surf leash **79**, p.11
surveyor **2**, p.4
swage block **35**, p.32
swallow **72**, p.25
swan **85**, p.25
sweetcorn **25**, p.18
swimmer **97**, p.17
swimming pool **145**, p.9
swimming trunks **21**, p.16
swing **51**, p.24
switch **100**, p.5
switchboard **18**, p.28
switch engine **21**, p.35
switch signal **19**, p.35
swordfish **70**, p.16
swordsman **69**, p.8
syringe **91**, p.37
syrup **69**, p.18

Tt

table **86**, p.6
tablecloth **85**, p.6
table tennis 97, p.11
table tennis bat **98**, p.11

tachometer 7, p.14
tackle box 68, p.24
tail 28, p.12
tailcone 61, p.14
tail fin 63, p.14
tailor 75, p.20
tailpiece 22, p.22
tailplane 65, p.14
tail puffer 29, p.15
tail rotor 22, p.14
tail skid 20, p.14
take-off board 22, p.8
tambourine 151, p.23
tambura 102, p.23
tandem 1, p.26
tangerines 50, p.18
tank 102, p.31
tank car 13, p.35
tanker 104, p.39
tank truck 79, p.27
tape measure 85, p.33
taper 34, p.21
tape recorder 9, p.36
tapestry 78, p.21
taps 40, p.6
target 120, p.11
target circle 89, p.11
taxi 78, p.29
taxi stand 70, p.29
tea 145, p.19
teabag 146, p.19
teapot 134, p.6
technical manager 131, p.37
teddy bear 94, p.31
tee 107, p.9
teeing ground 103, p.9
tee shirts 116, p.29
telegraph pole 46, p.24
telephone 100, p.7
telephone bell 8, p.4
telephone cable 64, p.28
telephone directories 101, p.7
telephoto lens 128, p.33
teleprompt 73, p.36
teleprompt operator 72, p.36
telescope 4, p.16
television 113, p.7
television aerial 1, p.6
television camera 65, p.41
television game 145, p.31
temperature chart 108, p.37
temperature gauge 8, p.14
tender 132, p.35
tennis 120, p.9
tennis ball 134, p.9
tennis court 123, p.9
tennis net 129, p.9
tennis racket 132, p.9
tenon saw 105, p.33

tenor drones 95, p.23
tension dial 82, p.33
tent 138, p.25
tentacle 74, p.16
tent peg 139, p.25
tent pole 133, p.25
test tube 39, p.30
thatch 103, p.21
thatcher 127, p.21
theater and lecture hall 19, p.38
theodolite 3, p.4
thermal insulation 56, p.40
thermometer 92, p.37
thermostat 121, p.5
thief 32, p.34
thigh pad 17, p.10
third stage 12, p.40
thread 94, p.33
throne 26, p.36
throttle lever 11, p.14
thwart 153, p.39
thyme 108, p.19
ticket collector 103, p.35
ticket machine 37, p.34
ticket office 26, p.34
tideline 19, p.16
ties 49, p.36
tiger 149, p.31
tile cutter 95, p.5
tiler 16, p.4
tiller 144, p.39
tilt 63, p.20
time keeper 58, p.8
timer 109, p.5
timetable 112, p.35
tire 153, p.27
tire levers 51, p.26
toad 82, p.25
toadstools 144, p.25
toaster 139, p.6
toast rack 145, p.6
toboggan 10, p.10
toe binding 137, p.9
toe stop 138, p.9
toe strap 145, p.39
toilet 46, p.6
toilet paper 38, p.6
tomahawk 60, p.30
tomatoes 30, p.18
tomato ketchup 158, p.19
tom toms 59, p.22
tongs 34, p.32
tool box 150, p.27
tool carrier 71, p.41
tools 1, p.12
toothbrush 119, p.6
toothpaste 121, p.6
top hat 34, p.36
torch 132, p.25
tortoise 73, p.25
totem pole 51, p.30

touch hole 28, p.21
tow bar 111, p.25
towel 39, p.6
towel ring 36, p.6
tower shell 38, p.16
tow hook 52, p.38
towing davit 112, p.39
towing lights 51, p.38
tow rope 118, p.9
tow truck 137, p.15
tow truck 78, p.27
toy stall 129, p.29
tracking light 49, p.40
track shoe 3, p.8
tractor 44, p.12
traffic light 127, p.29
traffic warden 89, p.29
T-rail 78, p.35
trailer 135, p.13
train driver 130, p.35
train guard 110, p.35
tramlines 125, p.9
tramp 125, p.29
trampoline 86, p.9
transceiver 78, p.41
transformer 140, p.29
transom 143, p.39
trash cart 80, p.29
trash hauler 90, p.27
traveler 141, p.39
trawler 54, p.38
trawl gallows 55, p.38
trawl net 56, p.38
tray 77, p.6
tread 34, p.4
treadles 7, p.32
treasure 87, p.31
trebuchet 20, p.21
tree 107, p.25
tree stump 143, p.25
trellis 61, p.32
tremolo arm 77, p.22
trench 143, p.17
trestle table 98, p.21
triangle 101, p.23
tricycle 2, p.26
trifle 100, p.18
trigger 8, p.20
trimaran 64, p.38
triple bar 71, p.10
triple jump 23, p.8
tripod 121, p.33
trolley 44, p.28
trolley bus 86, p.27
trombone 4, p.22
trophy 28, p.36
troubadour 82, p.20
trough 58, p.12
trousers 132, p.29
trowel 64, p.4
truck 92, p.27
trumpet 121, p.23

trumpeter 122, p.23
trumpeters 66, p.20
trunk 6, p.6
trunk (car) 136, p.27
T-square 65, p.4
tub 86, p.21
tuba 24, p.22
tubular bells 33, p.22
tug 47, p.38
tumble dryer 67, p.6
tuna fish 123, p.19
tunic 48, p.20
tuning pegs 85, p.23
tunnel 42, p.24
turbines 101, p.39
turbo-prop 40, p.15
turkey 86, p.13
turkey, roast 80, p.18
turn indicator 9, p.14
turning tool 18, p.32
turnip 7, p.18
turnstile 38, p.34
turntable 140, p.23
turpentine 58, p.32
turret 69, p.21
turtle 116, p.17
tutu 38, p.36
tweezers 160, p.33
twine 65, p.32
twist throttle 53, p.26
two-man bobsleigh 84, p.11
typewriter 137, p.31
typist 19, p.28

Uu

udder 26, p.12
ukelele 88, p.23
umbilical line 116, p.41
umbrella 15, p.16
umbrella light 125, p.33
umbrella stand 96, p.6
umpire 121, p.9
undercarriage 96, p.15
underfelt 94, p.5
underground entrance 31, p.34
underground train 53, p.35
underground train map 49, p.34
underpass 148, p.29
underseat bag stowage 70, p.41
underwater camera 124, p.17
uniform 48, p.36

universal joint **134**, p.27
Uranus **142**, p.41
utility pocket **88**, p.41

Vv

vacuum cleaner **54**, p.7
valley **27**, p.24
valve **25**, p.22
valve (tire) **44**, p.26
valve box **152**, p.29
van **77**, p.27
vase **48**, p.6
vaulting box **83**, p.9
vaulting horse **78**, p.9
vegetable marrow **6**, p.18
vegetables 1, p.18
vegetable stall **128**, p.29
veil **36**, p.36
vending machine **51**, p.34
ventilation pipe **107**, p.5
ventilation shaft **46**, p.34
Venus **134**, p.41
vibraphone **99**, p.23
vice **29**, p.32
video controler **133**, p.37
video control room **132**, p.37
video mixer **126**, p.37
video tape recorder **113**, p.37
viewfinder **118**, p.37
village **38**, p.24
vintage car **75**, p.27
viola **21**, p.22
viola players **47**, p.22
violin **17**, p.22
violin bow **19**, p.22
violinists **46**, p.22
visitor **98**, p.37
visor **68**, p.26

Ww

waistcoat **55**, p.36
waiter **93**, p.35

waiting room **111**, p.35
waitress **30**, p.28
walkie-talkie **140**, p.31
walking-stick **35**, p.34
walkway **10**, p.28
walkway **133**, p.5
wall **63**, p.12
wall bars **92**, p.9
walled garden **105**, p.21
wallpaper **155**, p.5
wallpaper brush **157**, p.5
wallpaper glue **154**, p.5
wall tie **59**, p.4
wall walk **146**, p.21
wand **9**, p.30
wardrobe **17**, p.6
warehouse **14**, p.35
warning horns **87**, p.34
warning light **105**, p.29
washbasin **42**, p.6
washing machine **78**, p.6
washroom **68**, p.15; **96**, p.35
wasp **87**, p.25
wastepaper basket **118**, p.7
waste pipe **116**, p.5
water bottle **49**, p.26
water bottle carrier **29**, p.26
water carrier **130**, p.25
waterfall **63**, p.24
water feed **122**, p.35
water fountain **30**, p.34
watering can **75**, p.32
water jet **77**, p.16
water jump **15**, p.8
water key **6**, p.22
water lily **79**, p.25
water melons **53**, p.18
water pipe **149**, p.29
waterproof watch **139**, p.17
waterskier **115**, p.9
waterskis **116**, p.9
water tank **134**, p.35
water trough **33**, p.32
water vole **17**, p.24
wave **111**, p.17
wax crayons **25**, p.30
weather chart **75**, p.36
weather reporter **74**, p.36
weather satellite **30**, p.40
weathervane **100**, p.13
weaver 1, p.32

web **89**, p.25
wedding dress **42**, p.36
wedge **148**, p.27
weighing machine **17**, p.35
weight **99**, p.37
weight belt **134**, p.17
weightlifter **35**, p.8
well **138**, p.21
wetsuit **137**, p.17
whale **122**, p.17
wheat **13**, p.12
wheelbarrow **69**, p.32
wheelchair **25**, p.36
wheelhouse **90**, p.39
wheel hub **147**, p.27
wheel rim **43**, p.26
wheel tapper **83**, p.34
wheel well **33**, p.15
whelk **47**, p.16
whip **61**, p.10
whisk **135**, p.33
whistle **23**, p.10
whistle lever **126**, p.35
white bread **127**, p.19
wicket keeper **28**, p.10
wigs **52**, p.36
wigwam **52**, p.30
windbag **92**, p.23
windbreak **13**, p.16
windlass **96**, p.39
wind machine **119**, p.33
windmill **25**, p.24
wind-on lever **110**, p.33
window **112**, p.7
window bars **84**, p.5
window box **59**, p.7
window cleaner **71**, p.29
window dresser **83**, p.29
window frame **125**, p.5
window pane **129**, p.5
windshield **121**, p.27
windshield wiper **67**, p.35
windsock **78**, p.15
windsurfer **96**, p.17
wine **142**, p.19
wine cellar **24**, p.38
wing **22**, p.16
wing mirror **112**, p.27
wing tip **77**, p.15
winner **13**, p.8
winning peg **127**, p.11
winning post **64**, p.10
wiremesh wheel **66**, p.41
wire stripper **89**, p.5

witch **12**, p.30
wizard **84**, p.31
wolf **157**, p.31
woman **66**, p.28
wood block **96**, p.23
woodcutter **126**, p.21
wooden spoons **148**, p.33
woodwind **41**, p.22
wool **100**, p.31
workbench **139**, p.5
workman **12**, p.4
workshop **110**, p.13
worktop **70**, p.6
woven cloth **4**, p.32
wrench **81**, p.4
wrestler **37**, p.8
wrestling boots **36**, p.8
writer **5**, p.36

Xx

xylophone **34**, p.22

Yy

yarn **8**, p.32
yaw thrusters **23**, p.40
yoghurt **167**, p.19

Zz

zebra **78**, p.30
zither **105**, p.23
zoom lens **116**, p.37
zucchini **10**, p.18